MARRIAGE

Who?

When?

Why?

DAVID KNOX

East Carolina University

PRENTICE-HALL, INC., Englewood Cliffs, New Jersey

Library of Congress Cataloging in Publication Data

Knox, David
  Marriage: who? when? why?

  (Prentice-Hall sociology series)
    1. Marriage. 2. Sex. 3. Free love. I. Title.
HQ734.K67   301.42   74–11101
ISBN 0-13-559336-0

PRENTICE-HALL SOCIOLOGY SERIES

*To Lisa, our daughter, who will
someday answer the who, when,
and why of marriage for herself.*

Printed in the United States of America

10 9 8 7 6 5 4 3 2 1

Prentice-Hall International, Inc., London
Prentice-Hall of Australia, Pty. Ltd., Sydney
Prentice-Hall of Canada, Ltd., Toronto
Prentice-Hall of India Private Limited, New Delhi
Prentice-Hall of Japan, Inc., Tokyo

Contents

IV
THE HUMAN RELATIONSHIP 149

Preface

In the mid 1960s I enrolled in the marriage course at a southeastern university. At the time, I had been dating a girl for two years. Although we had never talked of marriage, both of us assumed that it would occur. Drifting toward marriage seemed easy. The course shocked me into recognizing that our relationship was headed on a collision course. The only thing we had in common was the university community—the movies, card rooms, and parties. We were like two people in a bus station with tickets to different destinations. I passed the course and broke the relationship.

This book was written for the student in the marriage and family class who is concerned about his/her own marriage. Although based on research, it cuts through to the relevant issues of the person, the time, and the reasons for marriage. These are discussed as the who, when, and why of marriage. The theme of the book suggests that once we carefully consider who we marry, when we marry, and why we marry, we are no longer drifting toward marriage on some magical love wave. Rather, we have systematically considered the issues and alternatives regarding marriage and can approach marriage (if we decide to do so) with some assurance that our decision has not been left to chance and the prognosis for a successful marriage is good.

The theme of the section on "who" suggests that your decision to marry a particular person should be based on a consideration of common values, goals, and expectations of each other. You must raise the question and find an answer suitable to yourself and your partner. To rely on our courtship system to automatically sort out partners who are not compatible may be trusting fate too much.

Even when you have the "right" person in mind, the timing of marriage can be tricky. Reviewing the alternatives of remaining single, living together, or getting married shifts the traditional question from "When will we get married?" to "Do we want to get married?" "Do we want to live together first?" and "Is being single better?"

The "why" of marriage will influence the who and when. Analyzing your motives and those of your partner may help you to avoid making a lifetime commitment for the "wrong" reason. Although you may marry for a negative reason, you are not likely to stay married for that reason.

In the choice of a marriage partner, you are affecting your future happiness, that of your partner, and the home life of the children you may have.

If you carefully consider the who, when, and why of your marriage, the purpose of this book will have been achieved.

I would like to thank the following people who helped to produce this work: Jack Wright who guided me through the bewildering process of mate selection to a fantastic wife; Buford Rhea who encouraged the rethinking of several issues which often appear clear cut; Mary Wallace who stripped many of the biased statements from the manuscript; Barbara Von Hofe who corrected the bad grammar in an earlier draft and who emphasized the value of transitions; David Mace who encouraged the development of the manuscript; Frances who critically evaluated each chapter; and Jackie Joyner and Mae Allen who collaborated in typing the manuscript.

D. K.
Greenville, North Carolina

I

WHO?

*. . . many other bodies exist around mine,
of which some are to be avoided, and others
sought after.*

DESCARTES, Meditations

Marriage involves the greatest time commitment to another person you will make in your life. Your previous dating partner becomes your lifetime companion in sleeping, eating, recreation, and, possibly, child rearing. In no other relationship will you invest as much of yourself as in the marriage relationship.

Although you could have an enjoyable marriage with many people, you are not suited for all. Likewise, all persons are not suited for you. Part I deals with assessing the degree to which you and your partner are suited for each other. An understanding of yourself, your partner, and your relationship, coupled with your making decisions based on this information, will increase the chance of an enjoyable life together.

1

You

> *No man can completely know another, but by knowing himself, which is the utmost extent of human wisdom.*
>
> SAMUEL JOHNSON

Should you marry, you will take all of you to marriage. Not just love feelings for your partner and the belief that your relationship will succeed, but years of learning experiences. These experiences have resulted in a self-concept, a way of relating to other people, a philosophy of life, and certain values. These factors, as well as the impact of your parents and formal education on your development, comprise the focus of this chapter. As a result of considering these phenomena, you may better understand yourself and the type of person you may be asking someone else to marry.

SELF

Sociologists, psychologists, and philosophers continue to debate the nature of the self. Descriptions include the social (roles), the physical (body images), the subjective (thoughts and ideas), and the objective (behaviors observed). Before reading the discussion to follow, take ten minutes to discover your self-image. On a sheet of paper, number from one to ten. Next, write ten words or phrases which answer the question, "Who am I?" (Kuhn and McPartland, 1954). Examples of words one person used in a self-description are: good-looking, single, sociology major, senior, lucky, intelligent, sensitive, humorous, Democrat, and Protestant. Your statements will be useful in identifying yourself—the self you take to marriage.

The Development of Your Self

You are a socialized adult in that you have internalized enough societal norms (stop at red lights; answer the phone when it rings) to function as an independent agent. Your acquisition of various skills (reading, talking, writing, driving a car) has been accompanied by your development of a self. The process through which you have acquired this self can be explained by two concepts: taking the role of the other (Mead, 1934) and the looking glass self (Cooley, 1956).

A child sees the world from only one point of view—his own.[1] In order to function in society, he must see the world from another's point of view (Piaget, 1926). When one begins to "take the role of the other," he observes how another person behaves. He then copies or mimics that behavior. A little boy who plays cowboys literally takes the role of a cowboy by shooting toy guns and riding a stick horse. However, this acting is done in reference to other people—Indians—who he imagines are after *him*. The end result of this process is that the boy comes to perceive himself (cowboy) as a social object to which other people (Indians) respond. Knowledge of the self comes through interaction with others. You have an awareness of your *self* because others have confirmed your existence by interacting with you.

Confirmation of your *self* carries with it an attitude or feeling about your *self*. Your self-concept can be defined in terms of the sentences that you tell yourself about yourself. It is the way you think about, view, or regard yourself. Examples of phrases you use to express your feelings to yourself may include: (1) "I am a good person," (2) "I am a good-looking person," (3) "I am an honest and kind person," or (4) "I am a dishonest and mean person." The first three phrases reflect a positive self-concept. They indicate that you are happy to be who you are and the way you are. The last phrase reflects an unhappy and disappointed attitude toward yourself.

---

[1] To avoid the awkward shifting of "he" or "she," the masculine gender is used. Exceptions are those situations where both the male and female points of view are explored. In all other situations, feminists and female readers are encouraged to read "she" for "he."

"Each to each a looking glass, reflects the other that doth pass" observed Cooley (1956). The looking glass self is composed of three elements: (1) our imagination of how we appear to others, (2) our imagination of others' judgment of that appearance, and (3) a feeling about that judgment. We develop a self-concept—a feeling about ourselves—as a function of the social mirrors other people hold up to us.

For example, when giving a class presentation you look into the eyes of other students to assess their reaction to you. You feel good or bad based on the feelings of approval or disapproval you see reflected in their faces. Empirical support for the looking glass self was suggested by Videbeck (1960) who asked thirty students to give class presentations. Half of the group were given positive feedback about their public speaking ability; the other half were given negative feedback. Each student was asked to rate his own performance. The results indicated that their feelings about their performances were consistent with the feedback they received. This study was replicated by Maehr, Mensing and Nafzger (1962) who reported similar results.

Sources of Your Self

We have noted that your *self* emerges from interaction with others. All people are not equally influential in contributing to your self-concept. Your parents are one of the most powerful influences in creating and maintaining a positive self-concept (Stryker, 1959). Freud contended that the first six years of life were the most important in the development of the adult personality (Coleman, 1964). These years are usually spent in intimate association with parents. To the degree that the young child feels that he is loved and wanted, his self-image is a positive one. He accepts his parents' judgment of his worth.

As the child matures, peers will have an impact on his self-concept. The too-tall or too-fat person may be nicknamed "skinny" or "fatso." Both labels carry a negative connotation which has a lasting effect on the individual's self-concept (Berscheid, Walster, Bohrnstedt, 1973). Victims of these negative body evaluations exercise to exhaustion and diet to near starvation as they seek the culturally approved body type.

Since reflections from parents and peers may be different, it is clear that there is no such entity as *the* self-concept. You have an array of self-concepts dependent on various social roles (student, lover, employee). As these roles change, so does your self-concept (your teacher may project one image of yourself and your lover, another). Hence, your self-concept is always changing; it is not static.

The *self* not only receives messages about itself, it evaluates the information. The mind is not merely a *tabula rasa* upon which experience writes; the mind selects, records, and evaluates inputs. For example, if someone tells you that you are a vile person because you are living with your partner, you may disregard that person's opinion. You may feel confident with your own values and screen out negative evaluations.

Your self-concept is important for two reasons: one, the attitude you have about yourself will influence the attitude you have toward others. Harry Stack Sullivan (1953), a leader of the neo-Freudian movement in American psychiatry, noted,

> The self may be said to be made up of reflected appraisals. If these were chiefly derogatory—then the self dynamism will itself be chiefly derogatory. . . . As I have said, the peculiarity exists that one can find in others only that which is in the self.

Your self-concept also has implications for marital happiness. Aller (1962) reported a positive relationship between marital happiness and a positive self-concept. He indicated that you must first feel good about yourself before you can expect someone else to do so. When you regard yourself as a worthwhile person, worthy of love and acceptance by others, you can allow someone else to feel positive about you. You cannot expect others to love you until you first love yourself (Rogers, 1951). A freshman art major said, "I'm a terrible person. No one could ever love me." This person must change his self-concept before he can expect (or will allow) someone else to love him.

A positive self-concept should not be confused with selfishness. To Eric Fromm (1956), the selfish person does not love himself too much, but too little. The selfish person is always trying to do everything and get everything for himself because he does not regard himself highly and, therefore, does not expect other people to do things for him or be his friend.

The Pygmalion Effect

The Pygmalion effect as related to the self-concept means that we behave in a way that makes the expectations of others come true (Rosenthal, 1973). If your parents expect you to make good grades in college, the probabilities are increased that you will do as they expect. Likewise, if the person with whom you are involved expects you to be late, jealous, or unfaithful, you are likely to behave as expected.

In one study, five male graduate students drew numbers to ascertain who would be first to take out the plain female graduate student in their social psychology seminar (Kinch, 1963). "Is it true," they asked, "that if we tell her for five weekends that she is attractive and desirable that she will eventually believe it?" For four consecutive weekends each of the male graduate students took Melinda out. Each evening she (unaware of the plan) was told how attractive and enjoyable she was to be with. By the fifth weekend, the remaining male graduate student could not get a date with her. Melinda had a "real" date. In effect, her self-concept had changed (through social interaction) from "ugly and undesirable" to "attractive and desired." She began to dress and act consistent with the expectations others had of her.

Those with whom you interact have expectations of your behavior. Identify the expectations others have of you. What is expected of you? By whom? When others have negative expectations of you, it is important that your subjective *self* intervene to determine the validity of the expectations. For example, a male was told by his parents, "You will never amount to anything." In spite of this negative evaluation, he graduated from Harvard Law School without parental financial assistance.

As this section ends, you are aware that your self develops through interaction with other people and that it is influenced by them. In the section to follow, observe the style of your interpersonal relationships.

OTHERS

Interpersonal interaction may be categorized as social strategies, movements, and patterns. These categories represent styles of establishing and maintaining interpersonal relationships. Consider these in regard to the way you relate to other people.

What are your major social strategies? Long-term strategies refer to such phenomena as social climbing or prestige seeking, maintenance of superiority, and conformity. While these represent general themes of relating to others, short-term strategies may include flattering, threatening, joking, or teasing (Ruesch, 1953).

Do you tend to move toward, against, or away from other people (Horney, 1945)? If you move toward people, you have a need for affection and approval. Your need to be wanted, desired and loved, influences you to get to know others on an intimate basis in order to establish a close bond of companionship.

If you move against people, you exploit them to achieve your goals. Your need to excel and to achieve success at whatever cost results in the theme, "What's in it for me?" This is a Darwinian perspective: only the fittest survive and the strong annihilate the weak.

Unlike moving against people, privacy and self-sufficiency is your goal if you move away from others. You will not allow another to "know" you. You are as detached and as aloof as some movie stars.

Edwards (1973) identified three additional patterns of social interaction: cooperation-seeking, instrumental, and analytic. The cooperation-seeking individual is characterized by receptivity to and understanding of the needs of others and a resolution of conflict through personal sacrifice. If you have adopted this interpersonal style, you regard people in terms of their warmth and friendly attitudes. For example, suppose you are looking for a certain campus building and see a group of students walking toward you. You might ask them as a group to help you find the building. As a cooperation-seeking individual, you are careful to observe how friendly and cooperative they are. In a one-to-one relationship you regard maintaining your relationship with another as the ultimate goal and do not allow petty differences to destroy it. Your attitude toward others is "keeping the peace."

In contrast to a cooperative style, instrumental interaction involves a preference for dealing with situations by structuring them, by relating to lines of authority, and by adhering to tradition and custom. The instrumentalist learns the rules of the game and plays it.

In the above example of asking a group of students for directions, as an instrumentalist, you would identify the eldest member of the group or the person who appeared to have authority. You would be less concerned with "warm and friendly" attitudes than with the directions. In a one-to-one relationship you would be primarily concerned with the rules of the relationship and who is right. For another example, if two students were roommates and one liked to leave the light on to study late, the instrumentalist would take the position, "You don't have the right to leave the light on late at night."

The analytic person is a combination of the cooperation-seeking and instrumental style. He deals with people and situations through an understanding of personal and situational cues. He also explores alternative courses of action. As an analytic person who asks for directions from a group of students, you would likely smile and exhibit cordial behavior to the group leader or not ask the group at all but find the building some other way.

In general, females tend to be more cooperation-seeking and males more instrumental in their respective interpersonal styles. Both sexes seem to be equally analytical (Edwards, 1973).

By now you have identified your strategies (long- and short-term), movements (toward, against, and away), and patterns (cooperation-seeking, instrumental, and analytic) of social interaction. The desirability of one style over another might be considered in terms of its consequences. Knowledge of your style might also assist you in assessing if the achievement of your goals (personal and interpersonal) is being expedited.

PHILOSOPHY OF LIFE

In addition to your self-concept and pattern of relating to other people, your thoughts and ideas can be categorized into a philosophy of life.

The following discussion summarizes several philosophical positions.[2] Try to identify those to which you have made the greatest emotional and intellectual commitment.

Pragmatism

"The pragmatic method . . . is to try to interpret each notion by tracing its practical consequences (James, 1907)." Students use the pragmatic method when they ask their professors, "If I don't come to class, will it hurt my grade?" The pragmatist loathes abstraction and insists on concreteness and facts. The world is seen through an "if, then" lens—if I do this, then that will follow.

Humanism

A Quaker prayer illustrates the humanist perspective—"I shall pass through this world but once. If there be anything good I can do or anything good I can say, let me do so now. Let me not defer nor neglect it, for I shall not pass this way again." The humanist is dedicated to solving human problems. Most American politicians strike a public posture of humanism. Since humanism is man-centered, it is often associated with a non-theological understanding of man. For the humanists, the proper study of mankind is man. Science, the arts, and music all focus upon man and the betterment of his world.

Existentialism

Existentialism places the emphasis upon "existence," or the inner, personal, immediate experience. Its focus is upon inwardness, and it seeks to rescue man from the dehumanizing forces working to process him into an "organization man." The phrase, "Tell me how you are experiencing life this moment," illustrates the existential concern with the here and now. The existentialist is concerned with the meaning of your reading this line at this moment. Past and future events are considered unimportant and absurd.

Nihilism

"It's all for nothing" illustrates the evaluation that everything ends in nothing and that life is meaningless. The nihilist sees the world as a giant golf ball rolling off into darkness and disappearing. All human events are viewed with a "so what" attitude.

[2] I would like to thank Dr. Ralph James, North Carolina Wesleyan College, and Dr. Jack Wright, Tulane University, for their assistance in developing this section.

There are four major attitudes toward belief in a supreme being or God. The first, *Theism,* posits that there is a God who intervenes in the affairs of men. Prayer is not a mental exercise but history is changed through the supernatural intervention of a God who opens Red Seas to fleeing Israelites and heals crippled children at the shrine of Our Lady of Lourdes. The *Deist* asserts there is a God, but his conception is that God created the universe, and manufactured it so that it runs by a set of mechanistic laws. Now, he just sits back and watches his creation operate. It is as though He wound up a clock and threw it into space. This position was especially attractive to intellectuals of the late eighteenth and early nineteenth centuries, such as Benjamin Franklin and Thomas Jefferson. The polar opposite of the Deist and Theist is the *Atheist.* To the Atheist, there is no God and man is alone in the universe. As the British philosopher and mathematician Bertrand Russell (1951) put it: "In the scientific world, all this is different. It is not by prayer and humility that you cause things to go as you wish, but by acquiring a knowledge of scientific laws." The *Agnostic* differs from the Deist, Theist, and Atheist by saying, "It is impossible to know if there is or is not a God." The prayer of an agnostic is: "Oh God (if there is a God), save my soul (if I have a soul)."

These categories, while not exhaustive, do represent several basic philosophical positions. Few individuals can be characterized solely by one perspective. Where such characterization is possible, the person may be quite dogmatic. An insistence on one point of view would be likely to interfere with maintaining an interpersonal relationship with a "non-believer."

In regard to your philosophy of life, you should be aware not only of your philosophical perspective but also the intensity with which you hold that view. Extreme dogmatism on any perspective may limit your interpersonal possibilities.

VALUES

Embedded in your philosophy of life is a system of values. In this section, we will review the nature of values and attempt to clarify your values. Barrett (1961) noted, "Without much dispute, most people would agree that values lie at the core of life and human action."

A value may be defined as a behavioral choice preceded by a subjective evaluation. This evaluation may have a cognitive base ("I believe marijuana is safer than alcohol") or an emotional base ("I feel that living together before marriage is wrong"). Some commonly held values are wealth, power, pleasure, prestige, education, sex, honesty, kindness, fidelity, humility, and generosity.

Sometimes you are expected to choose between values when one is incompatible with another. This is true with the values of honesty and kindness. For example, suppose your aunt gives you a record album of Lawrence Welk's "Twenty-five Musical Memories" and you are an acid-rock fan. If your aunt asks, "How do you like the new album I gave you?", how will you respond? Will you be honest and unkind or dishonest and kind? If you are honest, you may say, "Well, I really don't dig that cat." On the other hand, if your first value is kindness, you may respond, "I really like the album you gave me." If you are caught between the values of honesty and kindness, you may say something diplomatic such as, "There are some good songs on the album."

A systematic way to explore your values is to observe your behavior.[3] Table 1-1 will help you to identify your values by observing the amount of time you spend engaging in various behaviors.

Notice the column "Estimated Time." In this column, you should estimate how much time you think you spend weekly engaging in each of the behaviors listed. For example, how much time each week do you think you spend with the person you are dating? How much time do you think you spend studying, talking with friends, smoking pot, and listening to music? Write these estimates in the appropriate column.

To see if your estimates are accurate, you will need to record the amount of time you spend actually engaging in the various behaviors. If knowing how you spend your time is important to you, carry a pen and small notebook with you for the next week and write down everything you do throughout the week. For example, when you get up in the morning, write down: 7:00–7:20 a.m., got up, showered, dressed; 7:20–7:45, ate breakfast; 7:45–8:00, walked to class.

After you have kept your record for one week, add the amount of time you spent engaging in each behavior listed on the chart and record this in the appropriate column. As you look at the completed chart, you can compare what you think you do with what you actually do. Be aware that your values are often reflected by your behavior.

Behavior is only one index of value. The motives for your behavior might also be considered. You may spend a great deal of time "working" or "studying" because you need the money or want to avoid failing. One sophomore pre-med student admitted that he only dated a girl because she typed his term papers each quarter. Although he spent a great deal of time with her, it would be false to say that he valued or loved her. Rather, his value was turning in neatly typed term papers at minimum cost.

[3] I would like to thank Dr. Charles Madsen, Jr., Florida State University, for his influence regarding the use of a behavioral log to assess values.

TABLE 1-1   *Behavioral Time Chart*

My Weekly Behavior	Estimated Time (hrs.)	Actual Time (hrs.)	Difference
Communication			
Person involved with			
Spouse			
Parents			
Friends—same sex			
Roommates			
Classmates			
Other (Specify)			
Friends—opposite sex			
Roommates			
Classmates			
Other (Specify)			
Letters			
Telephone			
Occupational			
Cooking, housework			
Study, homework			
Class			
Job			
Other (Specify)			
Physical			
Recreational (Specify—hunting, fishing, dancing)			
Eating			
Sleeping			
Sex (Masturbation, petting, intercourse)			
Drinking (Specify—beer, liquor, orange juice)			
Smoking (Cigarettes, pot)			
Hard drugs			
Walking			
Driving			
Spending (Specify)			
Daydreaming			
Hobbies (Specify)			
Looking, reading			
TV (Specify programs)			
Movies (Specify)			
Reading (Books, magazines, newspapers)			
Nature			
Sports			
People			

TABLE 1-1   Continued

My Weekly Behavior	Estimated Time (hrs.)	Actual Time (hrs.)	Difference
Listening 　Radio (Specify) 　Tape-player (Specify) 　Records (Specify)			
Spiritual 　Church or synagogue 　Religious reading 　Prayer 　Other			
Time Alone			
Words (Number) 　Positive ("Thank you") 　Negative ("I hate it.") 　Profane (Specify)			

Another example is that of a female art major who only dated a certain male because he gave her a free ride home on weekends. Although he believed that she liked him (because she spent time with him), it was his car and free ride she liked. He discovered her real value after he sold his car. She refused to date him again.

An analysis of your behavior in the context of your motives will assist you in understanding your values. An awareness of these values may encourage you to continue, discontinue or modify your behaviors and motives so as to be more consistent with your ideal self.

PARENTS

Your parents have been one of the most significant influences in the development of your self-concept, the way you relate to others, your philosophy of life, and your values. They have also influenced your ideas about marriage through "modeling" (Ingersoll, 1948). This term refers to behaving in the same way that you observe someone else behaving (Bandura and Walters, 1963). For example, if you have observed your parents throwing verbal barbs at each other, you may feel that this is the usual style of adult marital interaction. Having observed this destructive interaction, you may argue with someone with whom you are involved in much the same way. On the other hand, if you have observed your parents politely discussing and resolving their differences you are more likely to engage in and expect this same behavior from your partner.

Through observing your parents' behavior, you have learned two sets of expectations: (1) what you will do in marriage and (2) what your partner "should" do.

A few weekends ago, my wife's parents visited us in our small apartment. As we sat down to eat dinner at 6:30, my father-in-law began to pile food on his plate; then he collected his silverware, and put them on a tray to take with him to the living room to watch the evening news on television during supper. His wife responded to his behavior by asking him if she could bring his iced tea to him. On a subsequent occasion, I had chosen to watch the news on television while eating. My wife's response to this behavior was positive. Where did my wife learn this behavior? Clearly, she had observed her mother's behavior over the years when she responded positively to her father leaving the table to watch television. My wife responded to me as her mother responded to her father.

This story was told in a university marriage class. A sophomore female majoring in economics blurted out, "You are a male chauvinist pig. My mother expects my daddy to eat at the table and to get his own tea if he watches television. I expect the same of my boyfriend." You will be quick to notice that the girl behaves toward her boyfriend as does her mother toward her father. You will respond to your partner in a way which is very similar to the way in which your parent of the same sex has responded to the other parent. In many cases, your behavior will be a blend of both parents (Broke, 1967).

Consider the behavior of your parents in terms of its effect on your behavior toward an opposite-sexed partner. How did your mother respond to your father and vice versa when one partner was late, when one partner forgot something, and when one partner wanted to do something the other did not? How did your parents express affection and hostility toward each other? How is your behavior similar to that of the same-sexed parent? Some mothers teach their daughters to hate men while some fathers teach their sons to exploit women. Through observing your parents' behavior, you can better understand the basis for some of your own behavior and your role expectations in marriage.

It is possible that you are not happy with the way your parents behaved toward each other. This does not mean that you are locked into duplicating their behavioral patterns. Instead, because you are aware of their behavior and have labeled it as undesirable, you can make a deliberate effort to behave differently toward your partner.

EDUCATION

Parental influences are often tempered by formal education. In this section, we observe the possible ways in which your education may modify your earlier learning experiences and suggest implications of this modification for marriage.

College (undergraduate and graduate school) provides an environment for learning new information, skills, and values. Learning new information (e.g.: beliefs are not innate but learned, the concept of race is suspect, and the world is more than 6000 years old) often results in less dogmatism, less prejudice, and less commitment to organized religion (Feldman and Newcomb, 1969; Jacobs, 1957).

The acquisition of marketable skills as an undergraduate is unusual. Although elementary and secondary teachers (upon graduation) may begin their profession immediately, their training is not unlike that of the general college student. Rather, undergraduate training socializes the individual and qualifies him for the training programs of private industry.

Such programs and graduate school often result in socializing (developing the techniques and attitudes appropriate to the role) the individual for a new role. In this role, he acquires another facet of self. He becomes a social worker, commercial artist, or computer programmer which involves a unique set of expectations and behaviors. For example, the role of the social worker requires social skills which are not important for the competent computer programmer. Education is crucial in orienting an individual into a specific social role.

In addition to providing new information and marketable skills (usually with graduate training), education may encourage the development of different values. Researchers are divided on this issue. While Jacobs (1957), Feldman and Newcomb (1969), and Burgemeister (1940) concluded that college does not change basic values, other researchers disagree (Webster, Freedman, and Heist, 1964; Arsenian, 1943; Whitley, 1933; and Huntley, 1965). Huntley (1965) noted that the observation of longitudinal data is the only accurate means of assessing value change. In 1961, he compared the value scores of 1027 graduating men with their scores as freshmen. He observed significant changes in their scores, particularly of students majoring in different fields. For example, a humanities major showed significant change in five of six values (theoretical, economic, aesthetic, political, and religious) whereas a social studies major revealed a significant change in only two values (aesthetic and religious).

One study indicated that female sociology majors (married to sociologists) were more likely to get divorced than females who selected other majors (Glenn and Keir, 1971). The investigators suggested that sociology tends to strip the female of her traditional values thereby jeopardizing the stability of her marriage. For example, one attractive female sociology graduate student wearing a T-shirt and jeans remarked, "The double standard (sexual permissiveness appropriate for males but not for females) is bunk. Females perpetuate it by letting males get away with it. If I see someone who appeals to me, I will go after him—married or not. Of course, I intend to be discreet, but I will get my cookies where I can."

Consider the effect education is having on your attitudes, values, and behaviors. The person you select (should you choose to marry) before receiving your training may not be the same person you would select after your training. For example, a couple married while the husband was a minister. After four years of marriage he began to attend graduate school to earn a Ph.D. in psychology. Over a six-year period his philosophical position changed from theist to agnostic to atheist. He had married a woman to act out the role of minister's wife—play the organ, bake Christmas cookies, and teach in Sunday school. He now wanted a "swinger." Conversely, his wife, who had married a minister, now found herself living with an atheist. The relationship became intolerable for both. They divorced.

This couple may be unusual. However, commitment to attaining increased education should be regarded as an event which may alter significant attitudes and behaviors. You might ask "How will my college major (and, possibly, graduate school) affect the values which are important for happiness in my marriage?"

SUMMARY

Love is an emotion you take to marriage. Your partner does not marry an emotion but a *self*. Your *self* has a self-image, relates to others with certain strategies and styles, sees the world through a philosophical lens, and has a hierarchy of values. These variables combine with the influence from your parents and formal education to create the person you are today.

In Chapter Two we will discuss the characteristics of the person with whom you may link your *self*.

STUDY QUESTIONS

1. Comment on the different ways in which your *self* may be defined.
2. Explain "taking the role of the other" and the "looking glass self."
3. Why is an understanding of your self-concept important?

4. What is the Pygmalion effect? How is it significant in your interpersonal relationships?
5. Identify the patterns of relating to others suggested by Edwards.
6. Comment on four distinct philosophical positions.
7. Define Theism, Deism, Agnosticism, and Atheism.
8. Explain the statement, "Behavior is only one index of values."
9. What two sets of expectations have you learned from your parents?
10. How may education have an effect on your *self?* How does this relate to choosing a mate?

BIBLIOGRAPHY

ALLER, F. D. The self-concept in student marital adjustment. *Family Life Coordinator,* 1962, **11**, 43–45.

ARSENIAN, S. Changes in evaluative attitudes during four years of college. *Journal of Applied Psychology,* 1943, **27**, 338–49.

BANDURA, A. and WALTERS, R. H. *Social learning and personality development.* New York: Holt, Rinehart & Winston, Inc., 1963.

BARRETT, D. N. Value problems and present contributions. In *Values in America,* edited by Donald Barrett. London: University of Notre Dame Press, 1961.

BERSCHEID, E., WALSTER, E. and BOHRNSTEDT, G. The happy American body: A survey report. *Psychology Today,* November, 1973, 119–23, 126–31.

BROKE, H. A family over three generations: The transmission of interacting and relating patterns. *Journal of Marriage and the Family,* 1967, **29**, 638–55.

BURGEMEISTER, B. B. The permanence of interests of women college students. *Arch. Psychology,* 1940, no. 225.

COLEMAN, J. C. *Personality dynamics and effective behavior.* Chicago: Scott, Foresman and Co., 1964, p. 414.

COOLEY, C. H. *Human nature and the social order.* Glencoe, Ill.: The Free Press, 1956.

EDWARDS, C. N. Interactive styles and social adaptation. *Genetic Psychology Monographs,* 1973, **87**, 123–74.

ELMS, A. C. and MILGRAM, S. Personality characteristics associated with obedience and defiance toward authoritative command. *Journal of Experimental Research Psychology,* 1966, **1**, 282–89.

FELDMAN, K. A., and NEWCOMB, T. M. The impact of college: Epilogue in *The impact of college on students,* Vol. 1. San Francisco: Jossey-Bass, Inc., 1969, 325–38.

FROMM, ERIC. *The art of loving.* New York: Harper & Row, 1956.

GLENN, N. D. and KEIR, M. S. Divorce among sociologists married to sociologists. *Social Problems,* 1971, **19,** 57–67.

HORNEY, K. *Our inner conflicts.* New York: Norton, 1945.

HUNTLEY, C. W. Changes in value scores during four years of college. *Genetic Psychology Monographs,* 1965, **71,** 349–83.

INGERSOLL, H. L. A study of the transmission of authority patterns in the family. *Genetic Psychology Monographs,* 1948, **37,** 227–302.

JACOBS, P. E. *Changing values in college.* New York: Harper and Brothers, Inc., 1957.

JAMES, W. *Pragmatism: A new name for some old ways of thinking.* New York: Longmans, Green and Co., 1907, pp. 43–69.

KINCH, J. W. A formalized theory of the self-concept. *American Journal of Sociology,* 1963, **68,** 481–86.

KUHN, M. H. and MCPARTLAND, T. S. An empirical investigation of self attitudes. *American Sociological Review,* 1954, **19,** 68–76.

MAEHR, M. L., MENSING, J., and NAFZGER, S. Concept of self and the reaction of others. *Sociometry,* 1962, **25,** 353–57.

MEAD, G. H. *Mind, self, and society.* Chicago: University of Chicago Press, 1934, pp. 364–65.

PIAGET, J. *Language and thought of the child.* New York: Harcourt, Brace, and Co., 1926, pp. 196–97.

ROGERS, C. R. *Client-centered therapy.* Boston: Houghton Mifflin Company, 1951.

ROSENTHAL, R. The Pygmalion effect lives. *Psychology Today,* September, 1973, 56–63.

RUESCH, J. Social technique, social status, and social change in illness. In *Personality in nature, society, culture,* edited by C. Kluckhohn, H. A. Murray, and D. M. Schnider. New York: Alfred A. Knopf, 1953.

RUSSELL, B. *The impact of science on society.* New York: Columbia University Press, 1951, p. 17.

STEINER, I. D. and JOHNSON, H. H. Authoritarianism and conformity. *Sociometry,* 1963, **28,** 21–24.

STRYKER, S. Symbolic interaction as an approach to family research. *Marriage and Family Living,* 1959, **22,** 111–19.

SULLIVAN, H. S. *The interpersonal theory of psychiatry.* New York: Norton, 1953.

VIDEBECK, R. Self-conception and the reactions of others. *Sociometry,* 1960, **23,** 351–59.

WEBSTER, H., FREEDMAN, M. and HEIST, P. Personality change in college students. In *College and character,* edited by Nevitt Sanford. New York: John Wiley and Sons, Inc., 1964, 233–42.

WHITLEY, P. L. A study of the Allport-Vernon test for personal values. *Journal of Abnormal and Social Psychology,* 1933, **28,** 6–13.

2

Your Partner

*Throughout history man has chosen to conceal
his authentic being behind various masks.*

SIDNEY JOURARD [1]

The good-looking neatly dressed man cried as he mumbled his story to
the psychiatrist. Infidelity, alcoholism, and divorce had created feelings of
depression and thoughts of suicide. To encourage his client to be more
positive, the counselor recommended that he go to the local circus which
was featuring a jubilant clown who guaranteed that he could make people
laugh. "I am that clown," the man replied.

Few people know your intimate thoughts and feelings about anything.
Like the clown, you have the amazing capacity to reveal or conceal selec-
tive aspects of your self. Others who say they "know you," only know
what you have allowed them to know.

When you become involved with another, it is helpful to be aware that
the person you come to know is only the person that you are allowed to
know. Your partner (like yourself) is withholding (not necessarily inten-

[1] From *The Transparent Self* by Sidney Jourard. © 1964 by Litton Educational
Publishers. Reprinted by permission of D. Van Nostrand Co. and the author.

19

tionally) certain aspects of himself that he thinks you may consider undesirable. In this chapter, you are encouraged to learn as much about your partner as possible.

You may have two hesitancies about critically analyzing a potential mate. First, you may believe that scientific objectivity is unromantic. You may feel that observing your partner's behavior and asking questions violate the principles of a love relationship. Second, you may fear that systematically analyzing your partner will provide information which may upset you and result in your deciding against the marriage. One brown-eyed home economics major said, "I don't want to spoil our relationship by analyzing it." A critical look at your partner need not destroy your relationship. It may enhance it by increasing your feelings of security about your partner.

You are encouraged to consider the person with whom you are involved in much the same way that you did yourself in Chapter One. This analysis will include a consideration of your partner's values, goals (personal and marital), education, parents, philosophy of life, self-concept, and special needs.

VALUES

One way to learn more about your partner is to identify his values through observing his behavior. How much time does he spend engaging in each of the behaviors you observed for yourself in Chapter One? If you believe it would be helpful for you to know how your partner spends his time, ask him if he is willing to observe his own behavior.

If he has the time and desire, give him a pen and notebook and ask him to record everything he does for one week and to note the amount of time he spends engaging in each behavior. While your partner is recording his actual behavior, estimate the amount of time you think he spends engaging in each of the behaviors and record it in the column "Estimated Time."

When your partner completes his record, add the amount of time he spent engaging in each behavior and record in the column "Actual Time." Next, note the difference between your estimate of his behavior and his actual behavior as illustrated below. (See Table 2-1).

A coed estimated the amount of time (in hour units) her steady date spent engaging in 43 different behaviors. After he gave her his completed log, she put the totals for each behavior in the appropriate column. Finally, she noted discrepancies ($>$ = more than; $<$ = less than). Through observing her partner's log, this coed concluded, "My dude spent about as

TABLE 2-1   Behavioral Time Chart

My Partner's Weekly Behavior	Estimated Time (hrs.)	Actual Time (hrs.)	Difference
Communication			
Person involved with	8	10	<2
Spouse	0	0	0
Parents	2	1	>1
Friends—same sex	16	14	>2
Roommates	8	8	0
Classmates	8	6	>2
Other (Specify)	0	0	0
Friends—opposite sex	2	2	0
Roommates	0	0	0
Classmates	2	2	0
Other (Specify)	0	0	0
Letters	0	0	0
Telephone	1	8	<7
Occupational			
Cooking, Housework	½	½	0
Study, homework	15	11	>4
Class	14	10	>4
Job	6	12	<6
Other (Specify)	0	0	0
Physical			
Recreational (Specify—hunting, fishing, dancing)	4	2	>2
Eating	14	15	<1
Sleeping	40	49½	<9½
Sex (Masturbation, petting, intercourse)	2	3	<1
Drinking (Specify—beer, liquor, orange juice)	7	6	>1
Smoking (Cigarettes, pot)	5	4	>1
Hard drugs	0	0	0
Walking	4	3	>1
Driving	4	4	0
Daydreaming	3	2	>1
Hobbies (Specify)	2	2½	< ½
Looking, reading			
TV (Specify programs) Sports	4	2	>2
Movies (Specify) War	4	2	>2
Reading (Books, magazines, newspapers)	4	0	>4
Nature	0	0	0
Sports	4	3	>1
People	1	1	0

TABLE 2-1   *Continued*

My Partner's Weekly Behavior	Estimated Time (hrs.)	Actual Time (hrs.)	Difference
Listening			
Radio (Specify) Music and Sports	8	6	>2
Tape-player (Specify) Music	0	0	0
Records (Specify) Music—popular	6	5	>1
Spiritual			
Church or synagogue	0	0	0
Religious reading	0	0	0
Prayer	0	0	0
Other			
Time alone	9	2	>7
Words (Number)			
Positive	7 words	3 words	> 4 words
Negative	50 "	60 "	<10 "
Profane	5 "	12 "	< 7 "

much time on the phone as he did with me. He gave me a vague answer when I asked him who he was talking to."

Although many of your estimates may be accurate, you may be surprised at some of the discrepancies. Over 150 students enrolled in a marriage course in a southeastern university exchanged records of their behavior with their partners (Knox and Patrick, 1971). Examples of their reactions to each other's behavioral log follow:

> She asks me not to cut any of my classes and to keep up with my studies, while she ignores all of her own obligations.

> I think too much of his time is spent drinking and he wants too much sex, which is good in some ways but bad in others.

> I drank Cokes for almost eight hours. When Stan (a physical education major) saw how much I drank, he told me I was going to ruin my bladder —physical fitness is one of his values.

> From reading Carol's log I have discovered that she is really a goof-off (although I was quite well aware of this fact anyway).

> I was extremely glad to discover the time we spent talking exceeded the time we engaged in sex.

He did not inform me that he had changed his insurance, but left it as a surprise when I read his log. It was a surprise, too, because it showed that he is not only accepting responsibilities but he is reaching out for them. He seems more ready for marriage than I thought.

I learned that she spends a great deal of time drinking, considering she is a female. Also, though aware of a girl's tendency to curse when among other girls, I did not realize it was to such an extent and quite often as vile as a boy's language.

I didn't realize that Frank drank so frequently and heavily. He does not indulge so heavily when with me.

In addition to comparing what you think your partner does and what he actually does, notice if his behavior reflects his stated value. For example, the sophomore male whose weekly behavior is reported in Table 2-1 said, "I enjoy a lot of music." His behavior demonstrates that he does like music since he listened to it for eleven hours one week.

As noted in Chapter One, it is inaccurate to equate behavior and value. Although what a person does is a fairly reliable index of what he wants to do (value), there are numerous exceptions. For example, the sophomore also reported working twelve hours each week. It is possible that he may loathe his job but need the money. Behavior must be observed in context.

On the other hand, people are often dishonest with themselves. Had the male referred to above said, "I am a religious person" yet engaged in no "spiritual" behavior, one might wonder about his sincerity. Likewise, the phrase, "I love you" has little meaning unless it is expressed in observable behavioral terms. One male majoring in business told his fiancée that he loved her. The next day he left for a weekend at the beach with another girl he had been secretly dating. In effect, he loved his fiancée so much he took another girl to the beach. Observe your partner's behavior to assess if it is consistent with verbalized values. Be aware of discrepancies between what he says and does.

GOALS

Personal

Your partner's values are often reflected in certain goals. It is helpful to know your partner's goals to assess your compatibility with these goals. A male who was majoring in criminology had the goal of becoming a classifications officer in the state penitentiary. His ultimate objective was to be warden. The girl he was dating, a music major, loathed his career goal and belittled him by saying, "Is working in the 'pen' the best you can do?"

While females have traditionally achieved their primary life satisfactions from a husband and children, more recent evidence suggests that today's woman wants it all—marriage, children, career. Only 2 percent of 1063 college freshmen who responded to the college student questionnaire noted that they wanted to be unmarried career women. A similar percentage said that they wanted to be married career women without children. Most saw themselves as "married career women with children" (Epstein and Bronzaft, 1972).

Although a female's stated goal may be to have it all (marriage, family, career), in the long-run, her career usually yields to her marriage. Viewing their own careers as subordinate to their husbands' is true of the married female physician, lawyer and educator as well as the secretary, waitress and telephone operator (Hubback, 1957; Poloma and Garland, 1971; Sommerkorn, 1966).

In one study of 52 professional women (physicians, lawyers, college teachers, etc.), Poloma (1970) concluded that these females had jobs, not careers. For example, one Ph.D. sociologist was offered the chairmanship of her department. She turned it down saying that she had achieved the level she wanted (associate professor) and that it would be difficult to balance the responsibilities of the chairmanship with her home and marriage responsibilities. A male would more likely accept the chairmanship without considering its possible effect on his marriage.

The orientation of the female toward marriage and the family is also illustrated by observing the number of married part-time workers. In medicine, women physicians tend to work fewer hours than their male colleagues (Powers, Parmelle, and Wissenfelder, 1969). In academia, women with their Ph.D.'s are more likely to work part-time and reveal family responsibilities as the reason (Simon, Clark, and Galway, 1967). Among female social workers, there is a greater demand for part-time than for full-time employment (McFarlane, 1968; Tropman, 1968; and Lewin, 1962).

Marriage as the first priority among females is also illustrated by an inverse relationship between career plans and romantic attachments which was observed by Almquist and Angrist (1970) and Angrist (1970). Their longitudinal four-year study revealed that females' career aspirations waned after they became engaged or pinned.

Some females do not need marriage as a prerequisite for happiness. Rather, marriage is seen as restricting their options. The single life style will be considered in detail in Chapter Seven.

In regard to your future mate's career, it is important that: (1) you have a positive attitude about your partner's interest in a specific job or career, and (2) you communicate to your partner your positive regard for his (her) interest in that career. These factors are important since your mate will probably spend most of his time in that career. Day-to-day interaction with someone who has a career you deplore can be exceedingly frustrating.

Personal goals need not be limited to career aspirations. An anthropology major spent her summer driving to Mexico to "dig" among the ancient Aztec ruins. Although she did not plan a career in anthropology, she wanted to travel three months every year. Backpacking in Appalachia and canoeing in the mountain streams of North Carolina were like heroin to her. Of marriage she said, "If I find a fellow who can enjoy these things too, that's great. Otherwise, marriage would be foolish." Your consideration of a marital relationship with someone with these interests would imply your commitment to similar goals.

Marital

Having considered the career and leisure interests of your partner, you should give some thought to the type of marital relationship your partner expects and whether or not these expectations include children. Degree of desired involvement is the significant issue regarding the type of preferred relationship. Involvement may be minimal, limited, or maximal (Mace, 1972).

The first type (*minimum involvement*) is basically an agreement to exchange services. The male provides the income and performs the general duties of husband and father, but not to an extent that would seriously interfere with his vocational goals or his leisure interests. In exchange, the wife agrees to be sexually available, and to take care of the home and children (of course, the roles may be reversed). Beyond these behaviors, she is free to spend her time as she pleases. A marriage of this type makes few demands on the partners and there is every possibility that they may derive from marriage what they expect.

In contrast to this type of relationship, other couples choose to be more involved with each other. At this extreme—*maximum involvement*—the ideal involvement is similar to the "total relationship" described by Cuber and Harroff (1965). They refer to the marriage of a couple in which the husband goes home at noon at considerable inconvenience to have a quiet lunch and spend a conversational hour with his wife. This type of marital relationship is rare—about 5 to 10 percent of all couples (Lederer and Jackson, 1968).

Between these extremes is the marriage of *limited involvement*. In such a relationship, the partners enjoy sufficient individual freedom as well as sharing a reasonable amount of time together. Most couples could categorize their marriage as one of limited involvement (Mace, 1972).

Being aware of these types of marital relationships, what does your partner prefer? How compatible is this with your ideas about the relationship? An elementary-school teacher married believing that her partner shared her value of "all together togetherness." She was brutally awakened to her false assumption when he announced one morning, "I need some time of my own—you leech."

Aside from an agreement on the type of mutually desired marital relationship, some understanding regarding children may be important. Although most couples want children, some do not. Childless couples are particularly difficult to analyze since they are made up of two separate categories—the involuntarily and voluntarily sterile. Five percent of the population is involuntarily sterile and 13 percent voluntarily sterile (Bogue, 1971). The first figure is complicated by the unknown incidence of physiological sterility due to psychosomatic variation.

The folklore surrounding parenthood has been explored by LeMasters (1970). While babies have the capacity to increase an already happy relationship, they may also shatter a marriage (Dyer, 1963; Hobbs, 1965; LeMasters, 1957). One chemical engineer said, "I'm not cut out for children. They are too much trouble. I wish I could send them back."

How does your partner feel about children?

A geology graduate student married assuming that neither he nor his wife wanted children. Two years after marriage, she announced that she was ready for a baby (they had been living in the graduate married student apartments where she was surrounded by other young wives with children), and encouraged her husband to "get his head into the parenthood bit." He said that he had married believing that there would be no children; if she wanted to have children, the marriage was over. They divorced.

The problem of this relationship was the *assumption* on the male's part that there would be no children and the *assumption* on the female's part that "someday" there would be children. Discussing with your partner if children are desired, how many, and at what intervals may help to avoid unnecessary trauma.

EDUCATION

As noted earlier, education should be considered in terms of its possible effect on personality. Although it usually does not, education may modify your partner's values. This *suggests* waiting until your partner's education is complete to increase the probability that he will not radically change his basic ideas, values, and goals. Although there is no guarantee that these will not change after years of marriage, a college education accelerates value changes. This implies the wisdom of delaying marriage until your partner has "jelled."

Your partner's education may also affect income and job satisfaction. A college education is worth $60,000 (Withey, 1971) more over a lifetime than a high-school education. In addition, the college-educated person is more likely to have a job that is more satisfying and less accident prone (Withey, 1971). One study reported that job satisfaction and marital happiness were positively related for husbands. The happier the husband in his job, the greater his marital satisfaction (Ridley, 1973). These findings point out the positive effect education may have on marital adjustment.

PARENTS

Formal education is not the only source of influence on values and beliefs. As noted earlier, the way in which we learn most about marriage is through observing our parents' behavior. Our parents have had a subtle though impressive impact on our projected role relationship in marriage. During early development, the child tries to copy his parents' behavior. He wants to be exactly like them. This is followed by the adolescent period in which the teenager may actively rebel against any similarity between his own behavior and that of his parents. After the teen years, there is a return to the mimicking behavior that occurred prior to adolescence. Turner observed that the life style of an individual stabilizes by age 28 and is generally very similar to the model provided by his parents (Turner, 1972).

If you want to know why your partner behaves toward you as he does, observe the same-sexed parent. If you want to know the examples of marital interaction to which your partner has been exposed, observe the way the same-sexed parent of your partner interacts with the opposite-sexed parent. If your potential in-laws belittle and berate each other, the probabilities that your partner will engage in these same behaviors toward you in marriage are dramatic. The project in Appendix A suggests that you carefully observe the marital interaction of your potential in-laws. This will assist you in understanding the type of interaction between you and your future mate.

PHILOSOPHY OF LIFE

Using the philosophical categories presented in Chapter One, identify your partner's philosophical perspective. In addition, how does he rank the values of honesty and kindness? What are his values in regard to fidelity in your relationship? Is an extramarital relationship justifiable under any conditions? What conditions? If you were to have an affair, how would he respond? Divorce? Separation? Forgiveness? What?

On a ten-point scale, how similar would you rate your respective value systems? Zero indicates that your value systems are completely different and ten indicates that they are identical. Do you want your children to have your partner's values? Are you proud to have your siblings, parents, and friends know your partner's philosophy of life? Do you want to share your life with someone who holds this philosophy?

SELF-CONCEPT

What does the person you are dating think about himself? A glib answer might be "He thinks he's great." A closer look may reveal that your partner has low feelings of self-esteem reflected in his disbelief that you like him. On the other hand, your partner may have a healthy self-concept. It is important that your partner have a good concept of himself since a positive self-concept is associated with good interpersonal interaction.

You might ask, "Suppose my partner's self-concept is poor. What can I do about it?" You might assist your partner in identifying those characteristics of his personality (specific behaviors) which he defines as undesirable and in developing more appropriate behavior. In other words, if your partner feels that other people do not like him, try to identify specific behaviors in which he engages that "turn people off." These behaviors should be stopped. Likewise, identify specific behaviors that are conducive to close interpersonal relationships. These behaviors should be increased. Over time, these behavioral changes will be followed by closer interpersonal relationships and a more appropriate self-concept.

For example, Carol, an art major said, "Nobody likes me." When she observed the things she did that alienated people, she identified three negative behaviors: (1) Criticism of others. When talking to friends, she noticed that she made such statements as, "You're stupid if you think that way," "What's the matter with you?" and "You are a fat slob." (2) Punishment of approach behavior of others. When her roommate asked if she wanted to have a beer, she said, "I'm busy." (3) No eye-to-eye contact. When Carol talked with others, she generally looked down and talked to the floor.

Carol changed her behavior by complimenting rather than criticizing ("That's a good idea"), reinforcing rather than punishing the approach behaviors of others ("Let's go"), and looking directly into the eyes of those with whom she talked. The results, over a period of several months, were more friendships and a positive self-concept ("People like me").

SPECIAL NEEDS

You have been thinking about the person you are dating in a rather systematic way. You have explored his values, goals (personal and marital), education, parents, philosophy of life, and self-concept. Aside from these factors, you might consider special needs he may have which would affect the type of relationship you share.

Does your partner have any beliefs, expectations, or behaviors that you consider unique? For example, a university professor stated that he would only live in a home that had a cellar. He recalled that, as a child, his parents' home was destroyed by a tornado and that their lives were spared because of this cellar. For him, it was important that he marry someone who would not belittle him for his need to live in a home that had a cellar. This issue became relevant ten years later when they began to shop for a home in Kentucky. No homes had cellars in the area in which they wanted to live. After his wife selected a home that she particularly liked, a cellar was dug and paid for out of her part-time job.

Another example of a special need is that of a sophomore English major who was reared in a lower-class home. She said that throughout childhood her family was always poor—they had little to eat and never sufficient money to buy the things they wanted. She noted that this poverty had an effect on her desire to save money. She said that her first goal in marriage would be to accumulate $20,000 with her husband and put this in a savings account. Only after this amount had been saved would she feel comfortable having children. She married a man who felt as she did. They saved $20,000 in five years and then had their first baby.

Some physical difficulties may encourage an undesirable strain on a relationship. A diabetic requires food every 5½ to 6 hours. If sufficient food and insulin are not kept in the body at appropriate levels, death will result. The constant concern over food and insulin is an example of a special need. This does not imply that a diabetic cannot enjoy a happy marital relationship but does suggest that this potential difficulty be considered with some seriousness. Are you aware of your partner's special needs?

SUMMARY

Since premarital involvement is a potentially deceptive period, each partner must try to learn as much about the other as possible. For an effective beginning, analyze your partner's behavior to assess if it is consistent with verbalized values. Some people say one thing, but do another. What about your partner?

In addition to behavioral values, what are the personal and marital goals of the person with whom you are involved? Do you agree on the central issues of the wife's career involvement, type of preferred marital relationship, and children?

A knowledge of the educational, parental, and philosophical influences on your partner will help to explain his values, role expectations in marriage, and subjective nature. An understanding of these variables, coupled with an analysis of his special needs, will result in your getting past the superficial interaction which tends to characterize courtship behavior.

In Chapter Three we will analyze the social and psychological principles operative in bringing you and your partner together and consider your relationship from several theoretical viewpoints.

STUDY QUESTIONS

1. Defend the position that you only know about another person what that person has allowed you to know.
2. How may observing your partner's behavior assist you in identifying his values?
3. Discuss the current attitude females have toward career, children, and marriage.
4. Defend the statement that females tend to have jobs not careers.
5. Discuss the various types of marital relationships. What is the probability of achieving marital happiness with minimum versus maximum involvement?
6. What percentage of the population does not want children?
7. How are income and job satisfaction related to education?
8. Discuss the importance of knowing how the same-sexed parent of your partner relates to his or her spouse.
9. What is a helpful way to evaluate value similarity?
10. Give an example of how one's self-concept can be changed from negative to positive.
11. Give examples of special needs which may have an adverse effect on a relationship.

BIBLIOGRAPHY

ALMQUIST, E. M. and ANGRIST, S. Career salience and atypicality of occupational choice among college women. *Journal of Marriage and the Family,* 1970, **32,** 242–49.

ANGRIST, S. S. Change in women's work aspirations during college (or work does not equal a career). Paper, Ohio Valley Sociological Society Meeting, Akron, May, 1970.

BOGUE, D. Principles of demography. In Kenneth Kammoyer, *Introduction to demography*. San Francisco, California: Chandler Publishing Co., 1971.

CUBER, J. F. and HARROFF, P. B. *The significant Americans*. New York: Appleton-Century-Crofts, 1965.

DYER, E. D. Parenthood as crisis: A re-study. *Journal of Marriage and the Family*, 1963, **25**, 196–201.

EPSTEIN, G. F. and BRONZAFT, A. L. Female freshman view their roles as women. *Journal of Marriage and the Family*, 1972, **32**, 671–72.

HOBBS, D. F. JR. Parenthood as crisis: A third study. *Journal of Marriage and the Family*, 1965, **27**, 367–72.

HUBBACK, J. *Wives who went to college*. London: Heinemenn, 1957.

KNOX, D. and PATRICK, J. You are what you do: A new approach in preparation for marriage. *The Family Coordinator*, 1971, **20**, 110, 113, 114. Material in this chapter used by permission.

LEDERER, W. J. and JACKSON, D. D. *The mirages of marriage*. New York: Norton, 1968.

LEMASTERS, E. E. *Parents in modern America: A sociological analysis*. Homewood, Illinois: The Dorsey Press, 1970.

————. Parenthood as crisis. *Journal of Marriage and the Family*, 1957, **27**, 367–72.

LEWIN, T. F. The employment experience of married women social caseworkers: A study of one hundred graduates of the New York School of Social Work. Unpublished master's thesis, University of Washington, 1962.

MACE, D. *Getting ready for marriage*. Nashville: Abingdon Press, 1972.

MCFARLANE, PATRICIA. A study of the work patterns of selected married women social workers from the Columbia University School of Social Work. Unpublished master's thesis, University of Washington, 1968.

POLOMA, M. M. Role conflict and the married professional woman. Paper, Ohio Valley Sociological Society, Akron, Ohio, April 30, 1970.

POLOMA, M. M. and GARLAND, T. N. The married professional woman: A study in the tolerance of domestication. *Journal of Marriage and the Family*, 1971, **33**, 531–40.

POWERS, L., PARMELLE, R. D., and WISSENFELDER, H. Practice patterns of women and men physicians. *Journal of Medical Educations*, 1969, **44**, 481–85.

RIDLEY, C. A. Exploring the impact of work satisfaction and involvement on marital interaction when both partners are employed. *Journal of Marriage and the Family*, 1973, **35**, 229–37.

SIMON, R. J., CLARK, S. M., and GALWAY, K. The woman Ph.D.: A recent profile. *Social Problems*, 1967, **15**, 221–36.

SOMMERKORN, I. On the position of women in the university teaching profession in England. Unpublished dissertation, University of London, 1966.

TROPMAN, J. E. The married professional social worker. *Journal of Marriage and the Family,* 1968, **30,** 661–65.

TURNER, A. J. Huntsville-Madison County Mental Health Center, Huntsville, Alabama. Personal communication with author, 1972, and material used with his permission.

WITHEY, S. *A degree and what else?* New York: McGraw-Hill, 1971, p. 60.

3

Your Relationship

Grow old along with me!
The best is yet to be,
The last of life, for which the first was made
ROBERT BROWNING

The relationship with your partner was neither begun nor is it continued by chance factors alone. In this chapter, we review how several theories help to explain the initial attraction of two people and the subsequent development of a relationship. This analysis of mate selection emphasizes that human behavior is not random but guided by certain social and psychological principles.

For example, let's assume that several males and females are sitting in the campus Student Union the first day of the new school year. While some students are looking over the calendar of events for the fall term, others are reading the newspaper or playing gin rummy. Susie, a freshman, is sitting alone reading the newspaper. As she lowers it, she sees a male (John) across the room looking at her. She tilts her head and smiles. He smiles back. Their eyes lock. Susie smiles again as she slowly pushes up the newspaper so that only her forehead and shiny hair are visible.

A few minutes later, she walks toward the information desk. John meets her. They begin to talk. Their conversation results in an understanding that he will drop by her dorm later that night and they will go to the local movie.

While homogamy and value similarity theory may help to explain this initial interaction, the theories of complementary needs, role compatibility and exchange provide a way of understanding the developing relationship. These theories, as they relate to the heterosexual relationship, are the central points of this chapter. Try to analyze your own relationship(s) by using these theories.

HOMOGAMY

The homogamy or "like attracts like" theory of mate selection says that Susie is likely to date someone who is much like herself. For example, Susie is attracted to John who is a college student, two years older, and single. Were John a high school dropout, two years younger, and wearing a wedding ring, it is unlikely that Susie would be waiting in her dorm when he dropped by later that night.

Social class similarities are also significant in homogamous mate selection. Susie's parents are upper-middle class. They live in the expensive wooded section of her home town, have a full-time housekeeper, drink wine with their meals, and frequently have parties by their pool with a live band. John's parents are upper-lower class. They are separated. His mother lives in a third-floor apartment, and works as a checker in the supermarket. The family usually drinks iced tea at mealtime, then watches TV on their 5-year-old portable black-and-white set. Although Susie is not money or status hungry, she may feel uncomfortable and out of place in the surroundings John considers "natural."

The theory of homogamy suggests that you are attracted to others who share similar characteristics. These perceived similarities may be categorized as physical, social, and personal. Physical characteristics might include color, age, height, weight, and dress, while social similarities might refer to religion, education, and social class. Personal characteristics may include attitudes, values, and philosophy of life.

Although researchers differ in their evaluation of the relative importance of the physical, social and personal elements of homogamy (Hollingshead, 1950; Winch, 1958; Burgess and Locke, 1960; Trost, 1967; and Moss, 1970), all agree that homogamy factors are operative in defining those persons from whom a potential mate is selected.

A norm may be defined as an expectation of behavior that is associated with a system of rewards and punishments (Rhea, 1974). Cultural norms guide behavior. Your "choice" of a marital partner results in approval or disapproval from your parents, peers, siblings, and potential in-laws. Homogamy factors are operative not only because of personal choice, but because of social and cultural norms that reward certain choices and not others. Susie's parents are not likely to approve of John because he does not exhibit the social skills and behavior patterns of their social class. Her peers and siblings may ask, "Where did you get that bum?" On the other hand, John's mother may say to him, "Susie thinks she is too good for us. Find a girl more like our own kind."

Observe your own physical, social, and personal characteristics. Notice how these characteristics tend to define the characteristics of the people with whom you choose to become involved.

Research on the relationship between homogamy and marital happiness is inconsistent. While some studies suggest a positive relationship between similar personality characteristics and later marital happiness (Pickford, 1966; Cattell, 1973), others report no such relationship (Burgess and Wallin, 1953). Furthermore, it is possible that homogamy of attitudes is more a result of pair interaction than the initial meeting (Snyder, 1964). In other words, Susie and John will think more alike after several months of being together.

VALUE SIMILARITY

Aside from homogamy in general, the perception of similar values is a prerequisite for initial attraction and for the continuation of the relationship (Coombs 1961, 1966; Kerckhoff and Davis, 1962). In one study, the investigator gave differential feedback to 64 students about the degree to which a stranger shared similar values. Some students were told that the stranger shared their religious, political, and educational values while others were told that they shared none of these values. When the student perceived the stranger as having similar values to himself, the student thought him more intelligent, knowledgeable, moral, and adjusted. The student also reported having stronger positive feelings for the stranger when similar beliefs were held (Byrne, 1961). You will experience more positive feelings (love included) for people who share your values than for those who do not.

COMPLEMENTARY NEEDS

After basic physical, social and personal prerequisites are met (the field of eligibles is defined), Winch (1958) feels that the individual seeks that person who gives the greatest promise of providing him or her with maximum need gratification. In his famous theory of complementary needs, Winch suggested two types of complementariness: (1) The same need is gratified in both person A and person B but in very different levels of intensity. For example, one partner may be very dominant, the other also dominant, but less so. (2) Different needs are gratified in A and B. For example, one partner may have the need to be nurturant—to give sympathy and aid to a weak, helpless person—while the other has the need to receive that sympathy, care, and nurturance (Winch, 1967).

The relationship between Susie and John illustrates the second type of complementary needs. Since Susie was a freshman on campus, she did not know her way around. John was a junior and knew the local pubs, pinball spots, and hangouts. While Susie had the need for someone to take control and show her around, John had the complementary need—to do so. See if you can define the ways in which you and your partner complement each other.

Although the theory of complementary needs seems plausible, other researchers have failed to duplicate Winch's findings (Schellenberg and Bee, 1960; Murstein, 1961; Heiss and Gordon, 1964; and Trost, 1967). Some specific problems with the theory include: (1) Winch does not make clear the level of functioning of the complementariness. Is it overt and behavioral or covert and unconscious? (2) The criteria for determining if a need is complementary are unclear (Roscow, 1957). In essence, Winch has failed to adequately define the terms and parameters of his theory.

ROLE COMPATIBILITY

We noted earlier that each person takes a set of role expectations into marriage: expectations of his own behavior and expectations of the behavior of his partner. Since marriage involves day-to-day interaction of roles, Murstein (1967) hypothesized that couples select each other on the basis of role compatibility—the degree to which the expectations of one partner are met by the performance of the other. He analyzed the discrepancy scores of 99 engaged or involved couples and concluded, ". . . that couples do not choose each other by needs, but by roles (Murstein, 1967)."

The relationship between Susie and John illustrates role compatibility. Susie wants to have a career, to share the domestic responsibility with her husband, and to travel extensively. These expectations imply that John as a potential mate, must have a favorable attitude toward her career aspirations, perceive household chores (cooking, cleaning, washing) as a joint responsibility, earn a level of income that permits extended travel, and enjoy traveling. Murstein (1967) suggests that unless role expectations are met by a certain level of actual or predicted performance, the relationship will not continue.

EXCHANGE THEORY

The theories of homogamy, value, complementary needs, and role compatibility are not sufficient to explain the initiation and continuation of an involved relationship. "To posit value consensus or common interests as the prime basis for love and marriage exhibits only a tiny fraction of the iceberg and totally misses the dynamics of marriage formation and subsequent interactions" noted Scanzoni (1972).

Exchange theory provides the basis for analyzing the interaction of a developing relationship. This perspective is helpful for understanding all phases of the relationship from first meeting through marriage and for all categories of human interaction.

Bargaining Basics

Exchange theory in a developing relationship involves one partner providing rewards for the other in exchange for rewards from the partner. *Rewards* or *assets* may be defined as anything one partner has, says, does, is, or gives which results in the other partner's continued reciprocation of rewards. For example, John has a car, tells Susie he loves her, does nice things for her (takes her to parties and home with him on weekends), is a football player, and gives her records she likes. Susie evaluates each of these phenomena as a reward or asset. If she did not, John would have nothing to offer Susie and the relationship would not exist. A reward must be defined in terms of its effect on the other person.

Susie reciprocates these rewarding events by cooking for him at her apartment, telling him how much she enjoys going out with him, and turning down dates with other men. In addition, another of Susie's assets is her beauty. Walster (1973) noted that males like women whom other men want but can't get. The more desired by other men, the greater asset her beauty becomes.

In contrast to rewards or assets, *costs* or *liabilities* are those factors associated with the individual which may not be valued by others and which reduce the probability of interaction. Susie's freshman status and her major (biology) are liabilities from John's perspective. He would prefer that she be a junior majoring in sociology (his major). "I want a companion who knows what's going on in the world," said John. On the other hand, John's liability (aside from his social class) from Susie's perspective is his pot smoking. "He smokes too much dope," muses Susie.

The *profit* of the relationship for each partner is the reward minus the cost. If the reward remains sufficiently greater than the cost and if there is no alternative reinforcing partner available (Thibaut and Kelley, 1959) who offers greater rewards, the relationship will likely continue.

The balance of rewards and assets is continually shifting in a relationship. When one partner becomes over-involved (makes assets or rewards readily available to the partner without cost), feelings of exploitation or entrapment may occur (Blau, 1964). For example, if John takes Susie to dinner, to a rock concert, and to a sporting event, he will feel exploited unless he observes reciprocal behaviors on her part (talking to him and physical contact). Likewise, Susie may feel trapped and obligated to reciprocate John's behaviors. Neither feeling is compatible with a love relationship. The potential stability of a relationship can be assessed by the reward-cost ratio (Scanzoni, 1972). If both partners are getting maximum rewards at little cost, the relationship will be stable.

Bargaining Issues

With the exception of the male and female who are not interested in marriage, the content of most courtship bargains involves the exchange of sex for commitment. This is expressed by the female allowing greater sexual intimacy as the male increases his marital commitment. Although Susie is unwilling to allow John to fondle her on the first few dates (minimal commitment), she becomes less resistant as the relationship progresses toward marriage. Engagement frequently involves intercourse (see Chapter Eight) since the promise of commitment becomes more than whispered innuendos in the back seat of a '72 Ford at the drive-in movie.

The female bargains for commitment for three reasons: her self-esteem, her place in the economic structure, and the status of marriage. As will be noted in Chapter 8, traditionally females have been socialized to experience sex within a context of love. The labels of "tramp" and "slut" are frightening. To insure her feelings of self-worth, the female may demand some level of commitment. Ask a male if he wants to have intercourse, he says "Yes." Ask a female if she wants to have intercourse, she says "Who with (does he care about me)?"

Aside from protecting her self-concept, a commitment for marriage insures the female her place in the economic structure.

Last year, the football team at East Carolina University won the championship for the second consecutive year. As a tribute to the coach (who had been named "Coach of the Year" in the Southern Conference), the local merchants gave him a new station wagon which was driven onto the field and presented to him at half-time during the last game. After nodding in appreciation, he gave the keys to his wife who drove the new car from the field.

Since most females have jobs, not careers, marriage provides an immediate link with the economic system which translates into a car to drive, a place to live, and food to eat.

Finally, commitment to marriage is important since status among peers is associated with it. Although some coeds express the view that they do not want to get married now, the implication is clear that "sometime" is desirable. This is also true of most males, who prefer eventual marriage over bachelorhood.

Relationships often break up when the rate of exchange is uneven. In the usual relationship, a little sex is exchanged for a similar degree of commitment. If the female permits intercourse too early in the relationship, she may lose her bargaining power. The male learns that commitment is not necessary for sex and the relationship does not progress or terminates. In a similar way, if the male proposes marriage upon first meeting the female, she may wonder "What's wrong with this guy?" and break the relationship.

In the case of couples who live together with no intention of marrying, the relationship is sustained by a mutual exchange of companionship. Each partner supplies an intimate and accepting interpersonal context for the other in exchange for the same.

COURTSHIP SEQUENCE

Although bargaining occurs throughout courtship, it is not clear which theory of mate selection (homogamy, complementary needs, etc.) is operative at what time and to what degree during the development of a relationship. Several researchers have suggested ways to perceive the sequence of courtship (Reiss, 1960; Bolton, 1961; Kerckhoff and Davis, 1962; Murstein, 1970; and Lewis, 1973). They suggest that there is an orderly progression of a couple from no interaction with each other to a commitment to marriage. A synthesis of the above developmental theories follows:

"I Like What I See."
The Homogamy Stage

During this stage, the stimulus properties of the other must be sufficient to motivate interaction. The other must be perceived as sufficiently similar to the individual so that he predicts a positive response to a smile, a "hi," or other greeting. The perception of self and fear of failure are operative during this phase (Murstein, 1970). Specifically, if an individual sees himself as physically desirable, he will be more likely to approach an attractive person. Also, an individual is not likely to approach another—regardess of perception of self—if he fears failure. Persons who have just experienced a rejection in an interpersonal relationship (broken engagement, being stood up), may be fearful of initiating or becoming involved in a new relationship.

"I Feel Good About Us."
The Rapport Stage

As the couple share mutually enjoyable activities over time, reveal thoughts about themselves, and discuss topics of similar interest, pair rapport develops. A couple's history develops in the sense of "our song" and events are recalled with phrases like, "when we were there."

The rapport stage is the beginning of the emotional stage of the relationship. Each partner may respectively make reference to the relationship with emotional labels such as, "I love you" or "You make me feel so good."

Rapport is accelerated when one individual reveals some of his secret thoughts to another (Reiss, 1960; Worthy, Gary and Kahn, 1969). Such self-revelation results in the other revealing more about himself which results in the development of a unique relationship and speeds it toward greater intimacy.

"Am I Number One?"
The Commitment Stage

As the relationship builds momentum, there is pressure for commitment. At least one partner regards the rapport feelings as intensely satisfying and wants to insure a continued relationship. The commitment at this stage is less to marriage and more to pair exclusivity. At least one partner develops expectations of the other to disengage from other relationships as evidence of the seriousness with which the relationship and the partner are regarded. This may be an expression of a basic desire that we, individually, are number one.

The relationship may break at this stage. The pressure for exclusivity may be too ominous if one's style is to enjoy a number of intimate relationships at one time. When the partners share this perspective, however, the relationship continues and additional rapport may be developed.

"Here We Are."
The Progressive Involvement Stage

Relationship relaxation occurs when each partner is convinced of the other's sincerity (Waller and Hill, 1951). Although there is still a desire to make a good impression, the security of the relationship allows for more realistic interaction in which the partners may become increasingly transparent to each other. The significance of similar values, compatibility of roles, and the satisfaction of personality needs often becomes more important as the couple moves toward marriage. The phrase "we couldn't get going" usually refers to an assessment that value similarity, role compatibility, and need fulfillment were insufficient to maintain the relationship.

A commitment for marriage may or may not occur during the progressive involvement stage. While some will marry, others will end their relationship, and still others will live together. The meaning of living together in the context of courtship progress is discussed in detail in Chapter Five.

Sexual involvement transcends the four stages, with increased intimacy occurring in the latter stages. Pair bargaining also occurs throughout the stages with one partner frequently gaining control of the relationship. However, this control may shift as the emotional investment in the relationship also changes.

SUMMARY

In this chapter, we have briefly described the process of mate selection from several theoretical viewpoints. While homogamy and value variables are more operative in the early phases of interaction, complementary needs and role compatibility occur with increased involvement.

Bargaining occurs throughout the relationship. Each partner seeks to achieve maximum rewards at minimum costs. The relationship continues as long as the profit is greater than any other available alternative.

To learn more about yourself, your partner, and your relationship, complete the project on Assessing Your Relationship in Appendix A. Its purpose is to increase the levels of awareness you and your partner have about each other. By knowing more about each other you should be better able to evaluate your relationship.

STUDY QUESTIONS

1. Discuss how the homogamy theory of mate selection helps to explain various people you have and have not dated.

2. Give an example of how the theory of complementary needs is operative in an interpersonal relationship.

3. What is role compatibility? What did Murstein conclude from his research?

4. "The theories of homogamy, value, complementary needs, and role compatibility are not sufficient to explain the initiation and continuation of an involved relationship." Explain.

5. Discuss the terminology and concept of exchange theory as related to a love relationship.

6. Discuss how sex and commitment characterize the basic courtship bargain.

7. Why does the female bargain for commitment?

8. Explain, from an exchange perspective, couples who live together who are not marriage oriented.

9. Trace the various phases of a developing relationship. What theories are appropriate to describe each stage?

BIBLIOGRAPHY

BLAU, P. M. *Exchange and power in social life.* New York: John Wiley & Sons, 1964.

BOLTON, C. D. Mate selection as the development of a relationship. *Marriage and Family Living,* 1961, **23,** 234–40.

BURGESS, E. W. and LOCKE, H. J. *The family from institution to companionship.* New York: American Book Company, 1960.

BURGESS, E. W. and WALLIN, P. *Engagement and marriage.* Chicago: Lippincott, 1953.

BYRNE, D. Interpersonal attraction and attitude similarity. *Journal of Abnormal Social Psychology,* 1961, **62,** 713–15.

CATTELL, R. B. Personality pinned down. *Psychology Today,* July, 1973, 41–46.

COOMBS, R. H. A value theory of mate selection. *Family Life Coordinator,* 1961, **10,** 51–59.

———. Value consensus and partner satisfaction among dating couples. *Journal of Marriage and the Family,* 1966, **28,** 165–73.

GOULDNER, A. W. The norm of reciprocity: A preliminary statement. *American Sociological Review,* 1960, **25,** 161–78.

HEISS, J. S. and GORDON, M. Need patterns and the mutual satisfaction of dating and engaged couples. *Journal of Marriage and the Family,* 1964, **26,** 337–39.

HOLLINGSHEAD, A. B. Cultural factors in the selection of marriage mates. *American Sociological Review,* 1950, **15,** 619–27.

HOMANS, G. C. *Social behavior: Its elementary forms.* New York: Harcourt, Brace & World, Inc., 1961.

KERCKHOFF, A. and DAVIS, K. E. Value consensus and need complementarity in mate selection. *American Sociological Review,* 1962, **27,** 295–303.

LEWIS, R. A. A longitudinal test of a developmental framework for premarital dyadic formation. *Journal of Marriage and the Family,* 1973, **35,** 16–25.

McCALL, M. M. Courtship as social exchange: Some historical comparisons. In *Kinship and family organization,* edited by Bernard Farber. New York: John Wiley & Sons, 1966, pp. 190–200.

MOSS, J. J., APOLONIO, F., and JENSEN, M. The premarital dyad during the sixties. In *A decade of family research and action,* edited by Carlfred B. Broderick. Minneapolis, Minnesota: The National Council on Family Relations, 1970, p. 90.

MURSTEIN, B. I. A theory of marital choice and its applicability to marriage adjustment. In *Theories of attraction and love,* edited by Murstein. New York: Springer Publishing Co., 1971.

———. Empirical tests of role, complementary needs, and homogamy theories of marital choice. *Journal of Marriage and the Family,* 1967, **29,** 689–97.

———. Stimulus—Value—Role: A theory of marital choice. *Journal of Marriage and the Family,* 1970, **32,** 465–81.

———. The complementary need hypothesis in newlyweds and middle-aged married couples. *Journal of Abnormal and Social Psychology,* 1961, **63,** 194–97.

PICKFORD, J. H., SIGNORI, E. I., and REMPEL, H. Similar or related traits as a factor in marital happiness. *Journal of Marriage and the Family,* 1966, **28,** 190–92.

REISS, I. L. Toward a sociology of the heterosexual love relationship. *Marriage and Family Living,* 1960, **22,** 139–45.

RHEA, B. Department of Sociology, East Carolina University. Personal communication, 1974.

ROSCOW, I. Issues in the concept of need complementarity. *Sociometry,* 1957, **20,** 216–33.

SCANZONI, J. *Sexual bargaining: Power politics in the American marriage.* Englewood Cliffs, New Jersey: Prentice-Hall, Inc., 1972.

SCHELLENBERG, J. S. and BEE, L. S. A re-examination of the theory of complementary needs in mate selection. *Marriage and Family Living,* 1960, **22,** 227–32.

SNYDER, E. C. Attitudes: A study of homogamy and marital selectivity. *Journal of Marriage and the Family,* 1964, **10,** 51–54.

THIBAUT, J. W. and KELLEY, H. H. *The social psychology of groups.* New York: John Wiley & Sons, 1959.

TROST, J. Some data on mate-selection: Homogamy and perceived homogamy. *Journal of Marriage and Family Living,* 1967, **29,** 739–55.

WALLER, W. and HILL, R. *The family: A dynamic interpretation.* New York: Holt, Rinehart and Winston, 1951.

WALSTER, E., PILIAVIN, J. A., and WALSTER, G. W. The hard-to-get woman. *Psychology Today,* September, 1973, 80–83.

WINCH, R. F. Another look at the theory of complementary needs in mate selection. *Journal of Marriage and the Family,* 1967, **29,** 756–62.

―――. *Mate selection: A study of complementary needs.* New York: Harper, 1958.

WORTHY, M., GARY, A. L. and KAHN, G. M. Self-disclosure as an exchange process. *Journal of Personality and Social Psychology,* 1969, **13,** 59–63.

II

WHEN?

How to speak, I know not;
I am fluttered with forebodings;
neither in the present have I clear
vision, nor of the future.

SOPHOCLES, Oedipus the King

As a single, heterosexual adult, three cultural alternatives are available to you: getting married, living together (with no legal commitment), or staying single. Each of these options is considered in the following chapters. Questions such as "Are married people really happy?" "When is the best time to marry?" and "What about college marriages?" provide the focus for Chapter 4.

Living together—its uniqueness, incidence, commitment patterns, problems, and consequences—is explored in Chapter 5. The single life—its freedom and its loneliness—is considered along with the research on the mental health of single adults in Chapter 6. The dominant theme of Part II is that each alternative (getting married, living together, or staying single) is potentially meaningful and enjoyable for some people. Living together and remaining single should be considered valid alternatives to marriage.

4

Marry Now?

The greatest sacrifice in marriage is the
sacrifice of the adventurous attitude toward life:
the being settled.

GEORGE BERNARD SHAW

Marriage is a dominant life goal for most people (Sirjamaki, 1958). The first third of life is spent in preparation for and anticipation of marriage. Pre-school children play "Mommy and Daddy." Teenagers dream of moving away from home and getting married, and their dreams most often come true. Whether this results in happiness is another issue. Since most people marry, it is reasonable to ask, "Are married people happy?" This and two other questions—"When is the 'best' time to marry?" and "What about college marriages?" are the primary concerns of this chapter.

HAPPINESS IN MARRIAGE

In regard to "How happy are married people?" the most accurate answer seems to be, "No one knows." The data on marital happiness in five major studies with samples ranging from 409 to 2640 reveal that 58

47

percent to 85 percent of the spouses questioned reported that they were happily married (Popenoe and Wicks, 1937; Terman, 1938; Burgess and Cottrell, 1939; Landis, 1946; and Landis, 1962). But these percentages, alone, are not very useful without considering the meaning of marital happiness and how it is assessed.

Marital happiness, like love, is almost impossible to define. Any definition is subjective, individual, and variable over time. While some spouses may measure happiness by the absence of conflict that occurs in the relationship, others may consider conflict desirable and necessary for a happy, viable relationship. Some spouses see jealousy as a sign of mistrust, while others see it as a sign of love. In regard to the variable nature of marital happiness, the terms "marital success," "marital adjustment," and "marital happiness" imply a state of the relationship that exists rather than a process that the relationship experiences. The marital relationship is in continuous flux, and the positive or negative subjective evaluation may change at any time.

Marital satisfaction is often assessed by administering a questionnaire to spouses. The questionnaire items ask about such things as degree of agreement (friends, money, life goals) and amount of shared activity (recreation, affection, sex). The items may also request a self-rating of the relationship (happiness now, happiness at an earlier time, predicted happiness in the future). It is presumptuous for any researcher to project "right" or "wrong" answers to any of the questions which appear on marital adjustment forms. For example, if a couple disagrees about friends, money, or life goals, does this imply that they are unhappy? Hence, the reliability and validity of the scales are questionable.

Marital adjustment scales have other problems. For example, it is difficult to identify the source of an individual's happiness (Lively, 1967). If a husband reports that he is happily married, is this a function of his wife, their flexible or inflexible relationship, their children, his job, their neighborhood, or some other factor?

Not only may sources of happiness be diffuse, there may also be a tendency to give socially desirable answers (Edmonds, 1967; Edmonds, Withers, and Dibatista, 1972). The evaluation of marriage is a private experience. Some spouses may complete an inventory to reflect an "above-average marriage" because they are hesitant to admit that their relationship is less happy than they had anticipated. They may also fear disapproval from the spouse if he or she, inadvertently, sees the completed form. Although researchers are careful to communicate that each questionnaire is anonymous, respondents frequently feel that there is some "secret way" to find out who they are.

A final problem in assessing the marital happiness of those who complete marital adjustment forms is that of discriminating between individual happiness and marital happiness (Spainer, 1973). When an individual describes marital happiness, is he talking about his personal adjustment to life and his *general* happiness, or is he describing his spouse and their particular marital happiness? Individual happiness and marital happiness may be quite different.

Whether or not married people are happy remains unknown. The layman's guess that "some are and some are not" is about as accurate as current research method͡ʳ ·;y will allow.

THE BEST TIME TO MARRY

Although there is no guarantee for marital happiness, most people marry. The question then is not whether to marry but when to marry. (Frequently, the "when" question is answered when the right "who" comes along.) Since marriage is the most frequent choice for adult heterosexual behavior, is there any way to increase the probability of having a "successful marriage"? Burgess, Locke, and Thomes (1971) listed 26 premarital factors predictive of marital success that were found valid in four or more studies. These factors, shown in Table 4-1, are mostly concerned with the background of the individuals involved in the relationship, not the relationship itself. For example, *any* person who has a good relationship with his parents, has some college education, is over twenty at the time of marriage, and has not been previously divorced has a greater chance of staying married than someone without these characteristics. This implies that if you do not have the "right set" of premarital characteristics, selecting a mate who does may increase your chances of "happiness" together.

Realizing that marital happiness is a vague concept dependent on a subjective, individual, variable evaluation, and being aware that such happiness can be predicted for individuals only on the basis of background characteristics, what does research say about the relevance of some of the specific factors identified in Table 4-1? The following paragraphs review four of these predictors and attempt to elicit why they may be important for marital relationships defined as "happy."

Age

A review of eleven studies correlating age and success in marriage reveals that early marriage is associated with, but is not necessarily the cause of, divorce and unhappiness (Stephens, 1968). Early marriage means before twenty for females and before twenty-two for males. The longer

TABLE 4-1   *Premarital Factors Predictive of Marital Success*

Premarital Factors	Number of Studies Reporting
1. Acquaintance: well acquainted, or over 6 months	6
2. Adaptability: good general adjustment	4
3. Age at marriage: 20 or older for women, 22 or older for men	7
4. Age differential: man older or the same age as woman	6
5. Attachment to father: close	4
6. Attachment to mother: close	4
7. Church attendance: 2 to 4 times a month	4
8. Church membership	4
9. Conflict with father: none or very little	5
10. Conflict with mother: none or very little	5
11. Discipline from parents: not harsh	4
12. Educational level: some college or college graduate	6
13. Engagement: 9 months or longer	4
14. Friends before marriage: few or several women friends	4
15. Happiness of childhood: happy or very happy	4
16. Happiness of parents' marriage: happy or very happy	7
17. Married by: clergyman	4
18. Mental ability: equal	4
19. Occupation: professional	4
20. Organizations: member of some	4
21. Parents' attitude toward mate: approval	6
22. Savings: some	4
23. Sex instruction: adequate	4
24. Sex, source of information: parents	4
25. Sex relations, premarital: none or only with future spouse	8
26. Sunday-school attendance: some and beyond childhood	5

From *The Family,* 4th ed. by Burgess, Locke, Thomes. © 1971 by Litton Educational Publishing, Inc. Reprinted by permission of Van Nostrand Reinhold Company.

marriage is delayed (into the twenties and early thirties), the greater the probability of having what others have defined as a happy, successful relationship.

Age *per se* is probably not the determining variable of success or failure in marriage. Rather, age is a yardstick which helps to measure emotional, economic, relationship, and value maturity.

Emotional maturity indicates a tendency to respond appropriately to situations. For example, if a husband or wife comes home late and drunk (or stoned) one evening, his or her spouse, if emotionally mature, does not consider these behaviors justification for divorce. The mature person has established a sense of personal, positive self-regard and will not become emotionally paralyzed or immobilized when a disappointment occurs. Spouses past the teen years generally have had more experience in observing, controlling and refining their emotional responses. They may respond to such a situation with an attempt to resolve the conflict in behavior and expectations rather than by becoming defensive, withdrawing from the marriage, or threatening divorce.

Economic maturity means economic security—the ability to support yourself. A couple who marry in their late teens often seal themselves into a low economic bracket. Although money does not produce happiness, it pays the light bill, keeps the refrigerator operating, and brings water to the bathroom sink. In addition, money permits you to cool your apartment in summer and provides a color television for viewing. If your training does not permit you to command a desirable salary, your physical, emotional, and social energy may be drained trying to pay for those things you define as necessities. If you delay marriage until you complete your training or until you have a stable source of income, you can enjoy the standard of living you desire and avoid excessive hassles over money.

Relationship maturity is probably the critical variable operative in a successful relationship. Relationship maturity implies that you have the skills to: (1) understand your partner's point of view, (2) make decisions as to how you might change your behavior consistent with your partner's expectations, and (3) reinforce your partner for appropriate behavior. In order for you and your partner to get along before and after marriage, each must feel understood by the other. This translates into the ability to explain your partner's perspective to him (her). For example, Tommy and Theresa see the issue of living together from different perspectives (she's against it). To work toward a resolution, Tommy should explain to Theresa exactly how she feels. "You feel that living together is wrong. Although you agree that you would like to live together, you would feel guilty about deceiving your parents." Theresa should then give Tommy feedback about the accuracy of his perspective of her position. She should also explain Tommy's feelings about living together to him to assure him that she understands.

Relationship maturity also implies that you analyze your own behavior to assess in what ways you are contributing to a problem. For example, if your partner is continually late to pick you up or to meet you, you might consider that you do not thank him for being on time (reinforce on-time behavior), rather, you always reinforce late behavior by talking about how late he is. This perspective is quite different from asking, "Why don't you care about me?" Hence, rather than ask the question, "Why did my partner do that?", a better question might be, "How can I encourage my partner to engage in the behavior I desire by changing my own behavior?"

Value maturity is another quality embedded in the positive relationship between age at marriage and marital happiness. Partners nearing their mid-twenties have usually completed their formal education and may have developed a system of values which is real to them. This is quite different from the college freshman who may change his or her values significantly in the next four years.

Although early marriages are less "happy," more prone to divorce, and have lower "marital adjustment" than marriage in the mid-twenties, the emotional and economic relationship and value variables embedded within the age variable may be the primary elements which determine marital happiness. Do you define yourself as emotionally stable? (Do you have your head on straight?) Are you economically secure? (Can you support yourself and someone else, too, if necessary?) Do you have the interpersonal skills to get inside your partner's head and communicate understanding? Do you understand how desirable behavior is created and maintained in a relationship? Have you developed a value system which serves to direct your behavior in a way which makes you happy? Advancing age does not automatically result in positive answers to these questions but it does allow time to develop your emotions, interpersonal skills, and values.

Length of Acquaintance

The longer you know your partner (the longer you date each other exclusively and the longer you are engaged), the better your chances of a "successful" relationship (Burgess and Cottrell, 1939; King, 1952; Locke, 1951; Locke and Karlsson, 1952; Popenoe and Neptune, 1938; and Terman, 1938). An absolute minimum is twelve months. Although there are successful examples of couples who have met and married within a short period of time, the evidence is in favor of a prolonged premarital relationship.

As with age, length of acquaintance is valuable only if certain experiences occur during the time you spend together. For example, one consequence of an extended relationship is the difficulty each partner has in hiding his beliefs, values, and goals from his partner. The first few days, weeks, or months of a relationship, it is relatively easy for partners to withhold undesirable aspects of themselves. However, as the amount of time spent together increases, it becomes more difficult to play the Dr. Jekyl and Mr. Hyde game.

The concentric circles below provide a way to observe the level of relationship exposure over time (Lazarus, 1971). During the first few encounters with someone, he is apt to allow you to get no closer than the

"D" zone. Inside the "C," "B," and "A" zones are his intimate personal thoughts, values, and behaviors. "I hate religion" (C zone), "Sex is dirty" (B zone), and homosexual experiences (A zone) are examples. Whether

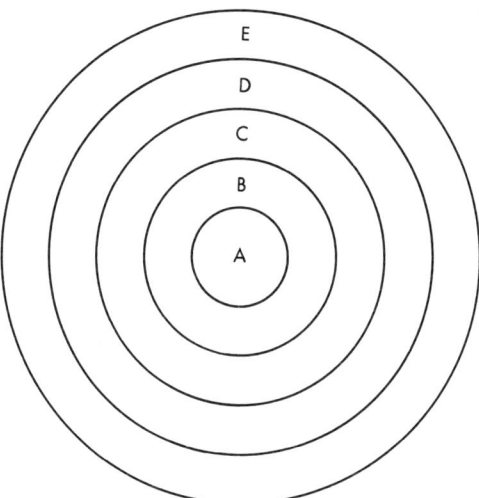

FIGURE 4-1   *You can assess the level of your relationship by defining your level of interaction. Levels "E" and "D" are usually revealed to strangers on first meeting (your name, class in school, college major). Levels "C," "B," and "A" involve increasingly more intimacy.*

it is desirable for you to get past the "D" zone of your partner is an individual matter. Some only enjoy a relationship in which all zones are open. One effect of such self-disclosure is a deepening of the love relationship (Reiss, 1960). Others prefer to overlook the issue of transparency in a relationship and enjoy each other without feeling pressured to "tell all."

In regard to your own disclosure, if you have been raped, feel guilty about earlier heterosexual or homosexual behavior or, have had an abortion, you may want to get these experiences in perspective. You might talk with an experienced counselor (rather than burden your partner with these events) and assess with the counselor the consequences of revealing or not revealing your previous experiences to your partner.

In addition to developing greater intimacy, an extended relationship may also be valuable since you and your partner can better assess each other's interests over a long period of time. Smoking pot, drinking booze, attending sports events or watching television may be behaviors which you or your partner enjoy on a frequent basis. It is important that each partner has a positive attitude about the other's interests or that he shares these interests.

An extended relationship will also increase the frequency with which you have contact with each other's friends. If you despise your partner's friends, you should more closely assess your partner since his friends are most likely very similar to him. This is true since we select as friends those who have qualities much like ourselves. Hence, if dating your partner for any length of time is to be of any potential value, not only must you get inside your partner's head and observe his behavior, you must also observe his willingness to be with your friends and your willingness to be with his.

Finally, an extended acquaintance will increase the probability that you will have disagreements and will allow you to observe how these disagreements are resolved: autocratic control, compromise, or acquiescence. In autocratic control, one partner categorically decides what will be done and imposes his judgment on the other. For example, if you want to have the wedding in a church, and your partner wants to have it in a meadow, he might demand that the wedding be in the meadow. You may become offended at this seeming indifference to your desires, or you may enjoy your partner's "taking control of the situation."

Compromise is an alternative to autocratic control. Each partner presents his point of view and a compromise incorporating both positions is developed. For example, you might agree to have two wedding ceremonies, one in the church and one in the meadow.

Relenting is a third alternative employed in resolving a disagreement. Either your partner would agree to have the wedding in the church, or you would agree to have the wedding in the meadow. Relenting differs from autocratic control in that the former may involve either partner. (Either partner may defer to the wishes of the other.) With autocratic control, the same partner always imposes his values when there is a conflict. An extended relationship allows you to disagree more frequently during which you can assess how your disagreements are resolved and whether or not you are comfortable with this pattern.

Education

The more education you have, the lower your probability of getting divorced (Glick, 1957; Glick and Carpenter, 1958; Locke, 1951; Monahan, 1961; Schroeder, 1938; Terman and R. Oden, 1947). Education is like a giant washing machine which shakes up your ideas about various phenomena (e.g., race, sex, and religion). As a result of your exposure to different ideas, you may begin to see the world differently. Because of this altered perspective, the person you choose to marry as a freshman may not be the same person you would marry as a senior. This possible change in choice of a marital mate is a function of: (1) your change in values, goals, and expectations which may have been altered by your educational experience, and (2) your partner's change in another direction. If you wait until you have completed your education, you increase the chances that your goals, values, and expectations of marriage will have "settled."

Also in favor of delaying marriage until after college, Margaret Mead (1972) states, "Under any circumstances, a full student life is incompatible with early commitment (marriage) and domesticity." She suggests two potential tragedies of marriage while in college. One, the tragedy of a "successful" marriage in which two freshmen meet, go steady, and cling to each other exclusively for four years. They do not take advantage of college as a broadening experience and show less vision as seniors than they did as freshmen. They may marry either as undergraduates or immediately upon graduation, have children in quick succession, and move to the suburbs to have more children, thereby supporting a choice before either has been differentiated as a human being.

Mead suggests the second kind of college marriage is more tragic. The girl drops out of school to support her husband's education. When he completes his degree, he feels as though he is living with an uneducated stranger and leaves her. Stephens (1968) admonishes, "Don't marry until you are out of school."

This does not imply that couples who meet and marry while in college do not report successful relationships over time. Neither does this imply that if you lack formal education you cannot and will not have a successful relationship. For example, one study found no relationship between educational and marital adjustment (Geismar and LaSorte, 1963) and another showed a weak negative correlation between level of education and marital adjustment (Hamilton, 1929). Although the evidence is in favor of completing your education before you marry and of getting as much education as possible, there is no consistent correlation.

Parental Approval

There is a positive relationship between parental approval and successful marital adjustment (Locke, 1951; Locke and Karlsson, 1952; King, 1952; Burgess and Wallin, 1953). Parental approval may be important since your parents know you best, may be more objective about your potential marriage partner, and may be more experienced in interpersonal relationships. However, it is not clear whether parental approval is important for these reasons, or whether parental objections generate a self-fulfilling prophecy effect. For example, parents who do not approve of their child's marriage may encourage their child to observe dissatisfactions in the relationship with the mate. A middle-aged mother told her sophomore daughter that her intended husband who was studying physical education was lazy. Later, the girl told her mother, "He is a lazy bum." Was the girl looking for what her mother taught her to see? Suppose the mother had said, "He will make you a good husband." Would the girl have looked for the qualities of a good husband? In addition, parents who disapprove of their son's or daughter's marriage may encourage him or her to leave an unhappy situation (and come home) rather than try to resolve the conflict.

It is entirely possible that you could have a "happy" marital relationship even though your background and that of your partner are not consistent with *any* of the factors predictive of marital success. One researcher said, "The best of the premarital tests predicts marital success as well as I.Q. tests predict school performance: Not very well, but worth considering as a warning when the score is quite low" (Udry, 1971).

COLLEGE MARRIAGE

About one-fourth (27 percent of the men and 19 percent of the women) of all students (predominantly seniors and graduate students) enrolled in United States colleges and universities are married (United States Bureau of the Census, 1970). This proportion of married student enrollment is a significant change from earlier years. Before World War II it was not uncommon for a college to automatically drop a student who married. The returning veterans who married and completed their education established the acceptance of marriage during college.

It is fallacious to speak of "*the* married college student." A look at married students sitting in almost any classroom reveals three basic categories. One is the person who has been married several years and is returning to complete study for an undergraduate degree. This is frequently the wife who married as a sophomore, dropped out to help finance her husband's education, reared children to school age, and is now returning to complete her degree.

The second type of married student is the person (with an undergraduate degree) who is returning to school for the Master's or Ph.D. degree. Both of these students are in contrast to the third type—the younger student who married just before or during college.

In 1967 over 3000 single students in 18 colleges were asked if they would marry while an undergraduate (assuming that they met the one they hope to eventually marry). Half of both the men and women said "Yes."

Nine-tenths of both men and women said they would marry if they were in graduate school (Landis and Landis, 1973). Marriage while in college is clearly an acceptable alternative, although most students prefer to wait until they have attained their undergraduate degrees.

Evaluation of College Marriage

Married students in several studies were asked, "Knowing what you now know, would you marry before finishing college, if you were unmarried?" (Landis, 1948; Christensen and Philbrick, 1952; and Eshleman and Hunt, 1967). Three-fourths of the couples said they would marry while in college if they had it to do over again. Although marital success among any group is difficult to assess, the available evidence seems to indicate that the majority of married students make a better-than-average success of their marriages. This is consistent with the premarital predictive factors discussed earlier in this chapter. Specifically, those with some college education and a "good" income have a higher probability of experiencing what they define as a "happy" relationship.

MARRIAGE NOW—SOME CONSIDERATIONS

Although marriage during college has a settling influence on the respective partners which often improves grades (Cohen, King, and Nelson, 1963; Glogau, 1963; and Schroder, 1963), marriage imposes certain limitations and responsibilities which should be carefully considered beforehand.

The Single Life—Gone

The role of the married college student is different from that of the single student. Marriage implies a time commitment to the partner and a decrease in time spent with single friends. As one student described it:

> Marriage is more different than I thought it would be. At first, I thought we would keep living like we were still single (playing cards in the student center, drinking beer downtown, staying out at night). But somehow, your single friends see you differently. They prefer running around with other singles. However, we have begun to spend more time with married people. We like it that way.

Where the desire to roam alone with one's friends is greater than that of being with the intended spouse, the advisability of getting married now should be re-evaluated.

Parenthood

Another possible result of a college marriage is the birth of a baby, which may shatter both the marital relationship and future professional plans. Increased expenses, upset schedules, and physical exhaustion may work against completing the degrees. In one study, childless married college couples tended to experience more marital satisfaction than did married college students who had children (Christensen and Philbrick, 1952).

Many couples use the pill or plan an abortion if the wife becomes pregnant to avoid a child during college. However, planning an abortion before conception is qualitatively different from deciding on an abortion after conception. One wife said, "Although we had planned to have an abortion if I got pregnant, I've changed my mind. To know that I have our baby inside of me is something that makes me want to keep it." Although the decision to get married and to have a baby should be separate decisions, frequently, they are not. Your feelings and those of your partner may change after conception actually occurs.

Money

Financial support for the couple need not be a problem when the parents of the respective partners continue to send money. Some parents, however, want to control parts of the relationship as a "return" on their investment. This "return" is often expressed in terms of parental expectations to come "home" on weekends, to write, or telephone frequently. Some parental expectations cover major decisions. For example, a father expected his son to live in the same town (after college) because he (the father) was financially supporting the married couple through college. Other parents may visit frequently since they are supporting the couple. Most couples are willing to accept the financial support but are ambivalent about fulfilling their part of the unwritten contract. Genuine independence requires economic independence. "He who has the gold, makes the rule, is the golden rule" (Sammons, 1974).

For the Wife—The End of College

In one study, one out of three women who dropped out of college said that getting married was a factor in their decision while, among males, one in ten mentioned this reason (Astin and Panos, 1969). If the female drops out while a senior, there is a 99 percent chance that she will complete her degree later on. If she drops out as a freshman, however, there is only a 5 percent chance that she will earn her degree (sophomore—20 percent;

junior—75 percent) (Womble, 1966). For freshmen and sophomores, marriage takes priority over educational achievement.

Several potential problems arise when the female stops her education to marry. In addition to never completing her degree and, possibly, reducing the chances of getting the job she wants,[1] the altruistic-wife syndrome (Cox, 1974) may begin. After several months, the wife, who spends her time typing in an office, filing manila folders, and talking to other dropouts during coffee break, becomes resentful of her husband who lives in a more enjoyable atmosphere. He spends his time attending college lectures, watching the girls in the library, and snacking with classmates in the soda shop. He usually studies at night, which his wife interprets as avoiding her.

When she can contain her resentment no longer, she says, "Why do you always spend so much time reading those books?" Since books and the academic pursuit may have become important to the husband, he may reply, "Why are you so dumb? You don't know anything except what those silly girls say at the office." Anger builds on both sides. The wife thinks as her emotions swell, "Has he forgotten that I quit school for him? Doesn't he appreciate the fact that I work to put him through school?" The result of this argument is mutual resentment and a strained relationship. He feels guilty because he has grown away from his wife and now defines her as a "dumb chick." She feels neglected and used.

Of course, this scene need not arise. Many spouses help put each other through school and enjoy their shared mutual companionship along the way. One college wife said:

> Being married and going to school is not so bad. It's tiring to be a wife in addition to being an employee and a student, but our relationship is fine.

SUMMARY

Marriage is one of three alternatives for adult heterosexual behavior. Although most people choose this option, their happiness compared to those who select the other options is obscure.

A successful marriage often occurs under certain conditions. Partners who marry in their mid-twenties, who have completed their educations, who have known each other for about a year, and whose parents approve

---

[1] On the other hand, a college degree is not a prerequisite for happiness or a job. The crystal ball of the social researcher clouds when he is asked to predict the effects of a specific decision (marriage during college) on the life satisfaction of the partners involved.

of their marriage have an increased chance of an enjoyable life together. Although a couple can marry under all the "right" conditions and still divorce, the probabilities of this happening are greatly reduced.

Marriage during college may present special problems in the form of premature curtailment of the single life, undesired parenthood, and limited finances. The relationship may experience specific strain if the wife terminates her education to put her husband through school.

Marriage should be kept in perspective. It is only one option, which can be entered into at any time after the legal requirements have been met. In the next two chapters, we look at these other options—living together and staying single.

STUDY QUESTIONS

1. What do most people report about their happiness in marriage?

2. Why is happiness in marriage difficult to define?

3. What did Edmonds and his colleagues discover about marriage happiness inventories?

4. Discuss some possible reasons why early marriages often result in unhappiness and divorce.

5. Why is relationship maturity necessary for marital success?

6. What is the minimum length of time you should know a person before marrying him? Why?

7. Why is it important to have disagreements before you marry?

8. How is education important in the timing of marriage?

9. What did Margaret Mead say about college marriage?

10. How may parental approval work for and against a marriage?

11. What percentage of college students are married?

12. Discuss the different categories of married students.

13. How do undergraduate married students feel about college marriage?

14. What issues should one consider before marrying while in college?

BIBLIOGRAPHY

ASTIN, A. W. and PANOS, R. J. The educational and vocational development of college students. Washington, D.C.: American Council on Education, 1969.

BURGESS, E. W. and COTTRELL, L. S. *Predicting success or failure in marriage.* New York: Prentice-Hall, Inc., 1939.

BURGESS, E. W., LOCKE, H. J., and THOMES, M. M. *The family*, fourth edition, pp. 344–95. Copyright 1971 by Litton Educational Publishing, Inc. Reprinted by permission of Van Nostrand Company.

BURGESS, E. W. and WALLIN, P. *Engagement and marriage*. Philadelphia: Lippincott, 1953.

CHRISTENSEN, H. T. and PHILBRICK, R. E. Family size as a factor in the marital adjustment of college students. *American Sociological Review*, 1952, **17**, 306–12.

COHEN, D. B., KING, F. J., and NELSON, W. H. Academic achievement of college students before and after marriage. *Journal of Marriage and Family Living*, 1963, **25**, 98–99.

COX, F. D. *Youth, marriage, and the seductive society*. Dubuque, Iowa: William C. Brown Co. Publishers, 1974.

EDMONDS, V. H. Marital conventionalization: Definition and measurement. *Journal of Marriage and the Family*, 1967, **29**, 681–88.

EDMONDS, V. H., WITHERS, G., and DiBATISTA, B. Adjustment, conservatism, and marital conventionalization. *Journal of Marriage and the Family*, 1972, **34**, 96–103.

ESHLEMAN, J. R. and HUNT, C. L. Social class influences on family adjustment patterns of married college students. *Journal of Marriage and the Family*, 1967, **29**, 485–91.

GEISMAR, L. L. and LA SORTE, M. A. Factors associated with family disorganization. *Marriage and Family Living*, 1963, **25**, 479–81.

GLICK, P. C. *American families*. New York: Wiley, 1957.

GLICK, P. C. and CARPENTER, H. Marriage patterns and educational level. *American Sociological Review*, 1958, **23**, 294–300.

GLOGAU, A. A teaching technique for a course on marriage and the family. *The Family Coordinator*, 1963, **7**, 25–28.

HAMILTON, G. V. *A research in marriage*. New York: A. C. Boni, 1929.

KING, C. E. The Burgess-Cottrell method of measuring marital adjustment applied to a non-white southern urban population. *Marriage and Family Living*, 1952, **14**, 280–85.

LANDIS, J. T. Length of time required to achieve adjustment in marriage. *American Sociological Review*, 1946, **11**, 674.

————. A re-examination of the role of the father as an index of family integration. *Marriage and Family Living*, 1962, **24**, 122–28.

————. On the campus. *Survey Midmonthly*, 1948, **84**, 17–19.

LANDIS, J. T. and LANDIS, M. G. *Building a successful marriage*, 6th ed. Englewood Cliffs, New Jersey: Prentice-Hall, Inc., 1973, p. 125.

LAZARUS, A. A. *Behavior therapy and beyond*. New York: McGraw-Hill Book Co., 1971.

LeMasters, E. E. Holy deadlock: A study of unsuccessful marriages. *Midwest Sociologist*, 1959, **21**, 86–91.

Lively, E. L. Toward concept clarification: The case of marital interaction. *Journal of Marriage and the Family*, 1969, **31**, 108–14.

Locke, H. J. *Predicting adjustment in marriage*. New York: Holt, 1951.

Locke, H. J. and Karlsson, G. Marital adjustment and prediction in Sweden and the United States. *American Sociological Review*, 1952, **17**, 10–17.

Mead, M. Is college compatible with marriage? In C. Safilios-Rothschild (ed.), *Toward a sociology of women*. Lexington: Xerox College Publishing, 1972.

Monahan, T. P. Educational achievement and family stability. *Journal of Psychology*, 1961, **55**, 253–63.

Popenoe, P. and Neptune, D. W. Acquaintance and betrothal. *Social Forces*, 1938, **16**, 552–55.

Popenoe, P. and Wicks, D. Marital happiness in two generations. *Marital Hygiene*, 1937, **21**, 218–33.

Reiss, I. L. Toward a sociology of the heterosexual love relationship. *Marriage and Family Living*, 1960, **22**, 139–45.

Sammons, R. A., Jr. Jefferson County Mental Health Center, Denver, Colorado. Personal communication, 1974.

Schroder, R. Academic achievements of the male college student. *Marriage and Family Living*, 1963, **25**, 420–23.

Sirjamaki, J. Cultural configurations in the American family. *American Journal of Sociology*, 1948, **53**, 464–70.

Spanier, G. B. Whose marital adjustment? A research note. *Sociological Inquiry*, 1973, **43**, 95–96.

Stephens, W. N. *Reflections on marriage*. New York: Thomas Y. Crowell Co., 1968.

Terman, L. M. *Psychological factors in marital happiness*. New York: McGraw-Hill, Inc., 1938.

Terman, L. M. and Oden, M. H. *The gifted child grows up: Twenty-five years follow-up of a superior group*. Stanford, Calif.: Stanford University Press, 1947.

Turner, A. J. Huntsville-Madison County Mental Health Center, Huntsville, Alabama. Personal communication, 1972.

Udry, J. R. *The social context of marriage*, 2nd ed. Philadelphia: J. B. Lippincott Company, 1971.

United States Bureau of the Census. School enrollment: October, 1970. Current population reports, Series P-20, Number 222, Washington, D.C.: United States Government Printing Office, 1970.

Womble, D. *Foundations for marriage and family relations*. New York: Macmillan Company, 1966, p. 144.

5

Live Together?

Marriage is forever. We can't go that far.
We only want a relationship—now, today.
Nothing is permanent.

A SENIOR COED [1]

The bond of love and trust which holds two
people together is much stronger than the legal
bond authorized by church and state.

LIFE MAGAZINE [2]

Their apartment is small. Record albums lie on top of their foam rubber bed, their books, and dirty clothes. They live together. They smile and shrug their shoulders, "It's no big deal." Their relationship developed from a first meeting in a sophomore history class, followed by a series of meetings during which they played pool, smoked grass, and attended rock concerts. They appear delighted with each other and say of marriage, "We don't need it. It's unnecessary."

Although some couples who live together fit this stereotyped "hippie" image, others do not. Gina and Gary share a modern, high-rise apartment across from campus. Their mahogany-stained shelves support textbooks and paperbacks in handsome array. *Newsweek* and *TV Guide* lie next to

---

[1] See page 70 for an overview of various commitment patterns of those who live together.

[2] "Unmarried: Miss McCann and Mr. Estridge Have a New Baby Girl" published in LIFE, April 28, 1972, p. 62. Copyright: LIFE Magazine, © 1972 Time Inc.

their photo album on a glass coffee table. Of living together they say, "It's what we both want for now." In this chapter, we consider living together as an alternative to marrying now and review the research on college couples who have chosen this life style. Issues to consider in making a personal decision to live together are presented at the end of the chapter.

DEFINITION

Living together, cohabitation, trial marriage, paramarriage, consensual union, non-marital units, unmarried marrieds, and living together unmarried [3] all refer to some form of heterosexual experience in which the unmarried partners share food and bed at a place each partner defines as "their" residence.[4] The experience of living together as currently expressed on the college campus is unlike marriage, one-night sex, or traditional dating.

LIVING TOGETHER IS UNIQUE

Unlike Marriage

Living together is different from marriage. There is no legal contract, very weak social support, and potentially divergent orientations of the partners for the future. As for no legal commitment, Ms. Wells, who has been living with her partner for several years, noted, "We feel that the freedom to re-choose each other whenever we want to reduces the risk of

---

[3] Robert N. Whitehurst, "Living Together Unmarried: Some Trends and Speculations." See Reference section for complete citation.

[4] Researchers have failed to define living together consistently. For example, Dan J. Peterman, Carl A. Ridley and Scott M. Anderson (1974) in their study on "A Comparison of Cohabiting and Noncohabiting College Students" defined living together as "Eating, sleeping, and socializing at the same residence with someone of the opposite sex;" John Hudson and Laura Henze (1972) in their "paramarriage study" defined living together as "two unrelated people of the opposite sex living together without being legally married;" and Eleanor Macklin (1972) defined four types of living together: Type A—Cohabitation: shared a "bedroom and/or bed" with someone of the opposite sex for four or more nights a week for three or more consecutive months; Type B—Longterm "Weekender" Relationship: shared a "bedroom and/or bed" with someone of the opposite sex for three or more months, but were generally together less than four nights a week; Type C—Short Term Intense Relationship; shared a "bedroom and/or bed" with someone of the opposite sex for four or more nights a week, but not for as long as three months (Note: Relationship could still be continuing and, in time, go beyond three months); and Type D—Periodic Overnight Relationship: shared a "bedroom and/or bed" with someone of the opposite sex for less than four nights a week and for less than three months.

separation. I have re-chosen Lee hundreds of times already and each time it is a real choice of stay or go" (Wells and Christie, 1971). Her commitment to Lee is internal (emotions and feelings) without the legal back up that married couples have.

Just as living together involves no legal commitment, social support for the relationship may be lacking. Couples who live together often have the tolerant social support of their peers and some university teachers. However, parents, landlords, and employers may view the relationship disapprovingly. Curtailment of college funds, eviction, and dismissal may be used to register this disapproval.

In addition to legal and social drawbacks, orientations of the partners for the future may be different. One study compared 31 engaged couples with 18 couples who were living together (Lyness, Lipetz, and Davis, 1972). Although both partners in the engaged group wanted to get married, females in the living-together group were more likely to desire the security of marriage than the males. Whereas many of the females were oriented toward marriage as a culmination of the living-together arrangement, only 3 of the 18 males in the living-together group reported any public or private decision to marry. The authors of this study noted that, "The living-together couples did not reciprocate the kind of feelings (of need, respect, happiness, involvement, or commitment to marriage) that one would expect to be the basis of a good heterosexual relationship" (Lyness, Lipetz, and Davis, 1972). Although partners may agree that marriage is not the goal of living together, when their expectations for marriage *are* different, the idea of the non-shared future may have a debilitating effect on the relationship.

Unlike One-Night Sex

Living together is also unlike the traditional shack job or one-night stand, since it does not appear to be sexually based. Most research suggests that the primary motive for living together is companionship—the desire to spend more time with the partner (Macklin, 1972; Croake, Keller, and Catlin, 1973). In one study, 97 percent of the living-together partners reported that they felt a "strong affection" for each other (Johnson, 1969). Although love may be a word used only in jest or in guilt between one-night lovers, persons who live together express or assume their emotional importance to each other.

Time commitment also separates couples who live together from the one-nighters. Some couples are committed to stay together until the end of the school year, others have an indefinite commitment (which may last a few days or a few years) and others, a permanent commitment. All of these time frames are different from the one-night commitment.

Unlike Dating

Living together is a radically different experience from dating. People who date are always prepared to interact with each other. The partners arrange to meet at a specified time to engage in a previously agreed upon behavior. Stan picks up Barbara at seven for a movie, a snack afterwards, and a slow walk back to her dorm. The dating event is highly structured and very predictable. Living together is more unstructured and haphazard. The partners interact with each other when they are *preparing* to go out with each other. Since they are together more frequently, they observe behaviors in each other which they probably would not see if they were just dating. The observation of these behaviors, which each partner previously has not witnessed, may affect the future of the relationship. For example, the female may not know that her partner sleeps in his underwear, rarely hangs up his clothes, and drinks a six-pack of beer every night. Likewise, the male may not know that his female buys very expensive clothes, despises cooking and cleaning, and rarely studies. One coed who was living with her boyfriend said, "You know, when you're dating you can say, 'Well, I'll be this way or this would happen when we're living together,' but when you're living together, it *happens* and you can't theorize any more," (Rogers, 1972).

Since attitudes and feelings are based on behavior, partners who live together generally have more information about each other which may affect these attitudes and feelings in a positive or negative way. This is different from partners who are only dating and who have limited information about each other.

THE INCIDENCE OF LIVING TOGETHER

Thirty-three percent of the undergraduate students at Pennsylvania State University and 26 percent of the undergraduates at Arizona State University reported that they had lived with or were living with someone (Peterman, Ridley, and Anderson, 1974; Hudson, and Henze, 1972).[5] Depending on the definition of living together and the sample studied, other research has reported the incidence of living together among under-

[5] Both studies were random samples. See footnote 4 for respective definitions of living together. In the Peterman, Ridley, and Anderson study, 1099 questionnaires were studied. This is the largest random sample of the living-together experience studied to date. It should be understood that living together is not limited to the college campus. However, empirical information on non-university unmarried marrieds is almost non-existent.

graduates to range from 5 percent to 54 percent.[6] Where the definition of living together is, "A heterosexual experience in which the unmarried partners share food and bed at a place each defines as "their" residence," the research suggests that between 20 and 30 percent of the students in most four-year universities live together at some time during their college careers.

Living together is increasing. Only 4 percent of the seniors at Pennsylvania State University in 1972 reported having lived with someone when they were freshmen as compared with 25 percent of the current freshmen women and 19 percent of the freshmen men who reported already having had cohabitation experience (Peterman, Ridley, and Anderson, 1974).[7] The differences in the Pennsylvania State University freshmen and seniors may be attributed to two significant factors: (1) residence hall policies were loosened at the end of the seniors' freshman year, suddenly making cohabitation more feasible; and (2) all of the present freshmen began studies at the University Park Campus, whereas many juniors and seniors spent their first year or two at branch campuses where many students live at home, or in more restricted residence halls. For other than the present freshmen class, the pattern of onset of cohabitation appears to be a gradual one, with usually about 10–15 percent of each class gaining a first cohabitating experience each year.

Living together as it currently exists on the college campus is likely

---

[6] (a) Charles Hobart, Abstract of Research in *Cohabitation Research Newsletter,* Issue Number 1, September, 1972, p. 4. Published by Eleanor D. Macklin, Department of Human Development and Family Studies, Cornell University, Ithaca, New York 14850. Dr. Hobart conducted a study in 1968 entitled, "Trial Marriage Among Students: A Study of Attitudes and Experience" on random samples of juniors and seniors at two Canadian Universities (Alberta and Waterloo) and freshmen and sophomores at a trade school. Five percent of these students reported that they had been involved in a trial marriage.

(b) I. S. Arafat and B. Yorburg, "On The Patterns of Living Together Without Marriage." Presented at The 1973 Annual Meeting of the Southern Sociological Society, Atlanta, Georgia, April 12, 1973. Twenty percent of their sample which was representative of the student body at a northeastern university reported that they were living together. The study was conducted in 1971.

(c) S. Y. Lautenschlager, "A Descriptive Study of Consensual Union among College Students," (Master's Thesis, California State University, Northridge, 1972). Ms. Lautenschlager analyzed 519 questionnaires from 11 classes in marriage and family relations at California State. Twenty-five percent had been involved in such a relationship previously and 10 percent were currently living together.

(d) E. D. Macklin, Abstract of Research in *Cohabitation Research Newsletter,* Issue Number 1, September, 1972, p. 8. Published by Eleanor D. Macklin, Department of Human Development and Family Studies, Cornell University, Ithaca, New York 14850. Dr. Macklin observed that 54 percent of the senior females in a random sample collected in 1972 had experienced living together using Type A definition as outlined in footnote 4.

[7] The authors of this study were careful to point out that most of the living-together experiences seemed to be "little more than greatly extended weekend sleep-overs." See footnote 4 for definition.

to continue. Several factors have combined to encourage this form of heterosexual behavior (Peterman, Ridley, and Anderson, 1974; Whitehurst, 1973; Jackson and Jackson, 1973):

(1) Permissiveness-with-affection has become a sexual norm (Reiss, 1967). (See Chapter 8.) Females who have intercourse within the context of a love relationship are not stigmatized and abandoned later on by the majority of other males. "Promiscuity" is a word reserved for females who sleep indiscriminately with several males with no regard to the love relationship. Since people who live together are regarded as caring about each other, sexual intimacy is legitimized.

(2) With the demise of the *in loco parentis* philosophy (the university stands in the place of the parents), universities have relaxed supervision and control of female students. "No hours" for women, coed residence halls, and off-campus apartments result in more heterosexual privacy which may involve living together.

(3) The availability of the pill and the IUD coupled with the legalization of abortion has reduced concern over pregnancy.

(4) Peer attitudes toward living together are supportive. Many college students regard living together as acceptable if there is a strong monogamous relationship between the partners. A mathematics sophomore said, "Everybody to his own thing." The favorable peer attitude toward living together makes it a desirable alternative for many college couples.

(5) Aside from changes in the norms of society, questioning of traditional values encourages the development of new courtship patterns. Some couples see marriage as an unhappy, outdated institution that is not working. They "hear" that divorce statistics give a marriage a 50–50 chance of surviving. (But Scanzoni, 1972, criticizes the misuse of marriage and divorce statistics. He states that between 80 and 85 percent of people who marry, stay married.)

Other couples see a husband and wife being shackled by marriage:

A great many skeptical bachelors listen attentively as their married friends say, "Well, I really would like to join you guys for the weekend but Nancy, ah, well, you know, she doesn't like for me to booze it up any more. And then there's the kids. If I left her alone with them all weekend, she'd give me a rough time for it next week. I'd love to go, but I really should stay home (Jackson and Jackson, 1973).

Increasingly, modern couples argue that a spouse no longer even knows what he *wants* to do, only what he should do, may do, must do. They say that the traditionally defined marriage tends to emphasize obligation at the expense of individual wishes. Avoiding the chains of duty, they seek a relationship held together chiefly by an emotional commitment to each other.

When asked why they thought cohabitation had become more common, respondents in Macklin's (1972) study mentioned: search for meaningful relations with others and the consequent rejection of the superficial "dating game"; the loneliness of the large university and the emotional satisfaction that comes from having someone to sleep with who cares about you; the widespread questioning of the institution of marriage and the desire to try out a relationship before there is, if ever, any consideration of permanency; and the desire to postpone commitment until there is some certainty that individual growth will be compatible with growth of the relationship. When asked why they personally started living with their partners, they emphasized the desire to be with that person and the fact that it was more convenient than living apart.

In commenting on these reasons Macklin (1972) noted,

> Given peer group support, ample opportunity, a human need to love and to be loved, and a disposition to question the traditional way, it seems only natural that couples would wish to live together if they enjoy being together. One might better ask: Why do students choose not to live together?

Most students report lack of opportunity and not yet having found an appropriate partner as the major reason for not living together (Macklin, 1972). The threat of parental disapproval and an internal feeling that "It wouldn't be right," may account for those students who have the opportunity and the partner but who choose not to live together. One student said:

> No matter how I present it, my parents would call it "shacking." I couldn't bear their disapproval. It wouldn't be worth it. I also feel that if a guy is really serious about me, he would want to marry me. I'm sorry, but living together seems like second best to me.

RESEARCH ON LIVING TOGETHER

How do living-together couples regard their relationship in terms of commitment for now and for the future? Who moves in with whom? What is it like? What are the problems? Are individuals who do live together different from those who do not in terms of background characteristics? Do couples who live together get married, break up, or what? The studies by Peterman, Ridley, and Anderson (1974), Macklin (1972), Hudson and Henze (1972), Croake, Keller and Catlin (1973), and Arafat and Yorburg (1973) provide empirical answers to these questions.

⋅   The commitment of couples who live together can be categorized in one of three ways (Cole, 1972):

1. "We love each other and plan to marry." These are highly committed (usually engaged) couples who see living together as a normal extension of engagement leading to marriage.
2. "We consider ourselves married already. The contract is unimportant." These highly committed (not engaged) couples see living together as an alternative to marriage or a kind of open marriage with formalized commitment.
3. "It's no big deal either way for us. We're happy today. We don't know about the future." These partners, who are marginally committed, view the relationship as tentative with no long-range plans of togetherness.

Some who criticize living together say that only in the committed relationship of marriage can maximum security and trust, which are prerequisites for mature love, exist. To find out the commitment patterns of couples who live together, Johnson (1973) examined a sample of nineteen married and nineteen cohabiting couples matched for age, childlessness, working status (male working and female in school) and time living together. When asked, "How long do you expect to stay with your partner," all of the married respondents felt "fairly strongly" about wanting to stay with their partners at least five years, while one-third of the cohabiting respondents did not intend to stay with their partners that long. Hence, the married couples were more personally committed to each other.

Social commitment was defined as the number of people who knew about the relationship and would disapprove if it broke up. The hypothesis suggested that more people would know of the marital relationship and would disapprove if it were terminated compared with the cohabiting relationship.

Results showed that the married couples were more socially committed since 95 percent of the cohabiting respondents named fewer than five persons who knew about their relationship and would disapprove whereas only one-third of the married respondents named fewer than five such persons.

The majority of Macklin's (1972) respondents defined living together as part of a "going steady" stage of the relationship rather than an engagement, even a tentative engagement. Most saw the relationship as one from which they derived considerable enjoyment but one they were unwilling to, or did not feel ready to, define as being oriented toward marriage. The vast majority reported that they had a "let's see" attitude toward the relationship. Marriage was not seen as a viable alternative to the present situation but was seen as something that may or may not occur in the distant future. The desirability of marriage could not be evaluated at the present time.

When living together is defined as "Eating, sleeping, and socializing at the same residence with someone of the opposite sex" (Peterman, Ridley, Anderson, 1974), the overwhelming majority of males (82 percent) and females (75 percent) report that the duration of the living-together experience (see definition of living together in footnote 4) is *less* than six months. In this study the authors concluded, "It appears that the vast majority of cohabiting experiences are not of the trial marriage or 'alternative life style' sort that have received so much attention in the popular press. In fact, a high proportion of them are little more than greatly extended weekend sleep-overs." However, most cohabiting relationships were defined as intimate or love relationships regardless of the length of time together (Peterman, Ridley, and Anderson, 1974).

In summary, couples who live together have various commitment patterns. While some couples are marriage oriented, most have a "let's see" attitude toward the relationship. Few regard it as a rather casual arrangement with no present or future commitment intended.

Live Together—How? Where?

When Macklin (1972) asked her students how they became involved in living together, they indicated that they gradually drifted into spending more and more nights together. The general pattern was for one partner to stay over one night with the other. In another week, to stay over two nights; in another week, three nights; until by the end of four months, they were staying together as often as four nights a week. If and when a decision with conscious deliberation was made, it was usually brought on by an external force such as graduation, room change (roommate moved out), or unexpected pregnancy.

In half of the cohabitation relationships, the partners did not spend every evening together. The female often returned to her own room one or two nights a week in order to see her friends and to allow her partner to see his friends. Even in those cases in which the partners lived together seven nights a week, practically all the females also maintained a room in the dormitory or sorority or in an apartment. Most went back once a day for a few hours to visit, get messages or mail, exchange clothes, shower, or study. Maintaining separate residences obviated hassles with parents, insured a place to live if the relationship did not work out, helped maintain contact with female friends, served as a good place to study, and provided the necessary storage space since it was often difficult to store both sets of belongings in the male's apartment. It is implied that the living arrangement which most frequently occurred was that in which the female moved into the male's apartment.

In regard to money, total pooling of finances did not occur. Rather, the female usually paid her way and maintained her own separate finances either because the couple could not afford otherwise or as a matter of principle. In regard to various self-maintenance chores such as shopping and laundry, the couple usually did these things together. However, there was a tendency for the female to assume greater responsibility for cooking and cleaning.

In essence, the living-together experience for college undergraduates is one in which the female usually moves in with the male after several months of dating; they share an increasing amount of time with each other but not to the exclusion of their peers; their finances are maintained separately; and their self-maintenance chores are often shared, with the female taking the greater responsibility.

Problems

Macklin (1972) observed that living-together relationships were not without problems. The major problem was parental. Because of fear of disapproval and unpleasant repercussions, more than two-thirds had tried to conceal the relationship from their parents.[8] Many indicated sadness at not being able to share this important part of their lives with their parents.

An emotional problem reported by many was the tendency to become over-involved and the resulting loss of identity. Macklin hypothesized that the manner in which this issue of dependency was dealt with would be a major determinant of the outcome of the relationship. One of the most uncontrolled variables in marriage is the different rates at which spouses grow intellectually, socially, and emotionally. If this "match" does not continue throughout the years, the partners often grow apart. Seemingly, this was one of the more difficult aspects of the living-together arrangement.

Sexual problems included differences over frequency of sexual activity, lack of orgasm, fear of pregnancy, vaginal irritations, feelings of sexual inhibition, and less satisfaction with sex as the relationship deteriorated.[9] In most cases (80 percent), the couples used some type of contraception.

Other problems mentioned were in regard to the living-together situation in which lack of privacy, lack of adequate space, lack of sufficient

---

[8] Concealment of the living-together relationship from parents was also found by Peterman, Ridley, and Anderson (1974); Croake, Keller, and Catlin (1974); and Lautenschlager, (1972).

[9] See Appendix C for a discussion on resolving sexual problems.

funds, or disagreement over money sometimes resulted in periods of dissatisfaction. Although these suggest the range of problems experienced by those couples who lived together, they were not described as serious problems.

The partners did not complain of problems experienced with the external community such as landlords, neighbors, employers, or student administrators.

Those Who Live Together and Those Who Don't

Peterman, Ridley, and Anderson (1974) compared the background, personal, and interpersonal characteristics of cohabitors and non-cohabitors. They concluded that cohabiting students differ little from their non-cohabiting counterparts in family and community background, or their levels of intellectual and emotional functioning. Hence, individuals who choose to live together, essentially, make the same grades, study the same curriculum, get the same financial suport from home, have similar proportions of parents who are separated or divorced, and come from the same size towns with equal frequency. The authors also concluded that cohabitors do appear to be highly interpersonally oriented in general and cohabitation is interpreted as a natural addition to their wide interpersonal base.

Henze and Hudson collected and analyzed data on a random sample of the student body (academic year 1971–1972) at Arizona State University. They observed that family background characteristics failed to differentiate between cohabitors and noncohabitors. However, personal characteristics in the areas of religion, life style, and drugs tended to distinguish the two groups. Cohabitors, compared to noncohabitors, were less apt to attend church, more likely to identify with a liberal life style, and tended to use drugs.

What Happens to Couples Who Live Together?

Among Macklin's (1972) respondents, a third of the relationships had dissolved (having lasted an average of four and one half months from the time they began staying together four or more nights a week), a third were married or planning to be married, and another third were still in the process of defining their relationship. In 80 percent of the cases, the living-together relationship was seen as both maturing and pleasant. The benefits included a deeper understanding of themselves and of their needs, an increased knowledge of what is involved in a relationship, clarification of what they want in marriage, and increased emotional maturity.

An example of positive student reaction to the living-together experience is this evaluation by a senior coed:

This is our second year together. The fact that we choose to stay together adds a sense of New Year's Eve excitement to our relationship. We love it. We don't want to spoil it by getting married.

In the Pennsylvania State University study, the authors concluded,

There is no immediately obvious negative effect of cohabitation, at least in terms of self-described personal adjustment or functioning as a student. If anything, cohabitation is associated with more positive self-attitudes and heterosexual relating (Peterman, Ridley, and Anderson, 1974).

Negative consequences are experienced by some. One female explained:

At first I agreed to live together because I thought we would grow closer together and would be married. It didn't work out that way. He never mentioned marriage and got angry when I brought it up. His indifference finally got to me so I moved out. I feel guilty and sorry about the whole thing. Living together is not for me.

Dr. James Rue, President of The National Alliance for Family Life, believes that the above described experience is too frequent. He noted, "For over 18 years of practice in marriage and family counseling, I have seen disastrous results of cohabitation among the unmarried" (Rue, 1973).

LIVING TOGETHER—DURING AND AFTER COLLEGE

The probability of the college student living with someone of the opposite sex is influenced by the absence of parental knowledge, the presence of peer support, and tolerance from the university community. These factors affect the trend toward living together during the college years, and, may affect its demise after college. Although some parents know of their son's or daughter's living together, most do not. The response of the parents who know tends to be more one of tolerance than of approval. It is the rare parent who will publicly acknowledge that his child, though not married, is living with someone.

Peers, as an important reference group, also have a tremendous impact on the tendency of students to live together. A coed returning to her dorm after living together with her boyfriend for four days may encourage her roommate to move in with her own boyfriend. If several of one's closest friends relate the joys of living together, the probability soars that that person will seek the same experience.

The university community encourages living together by looking the other way at dorm violations, establishing "no hours," and allowing university women to live off campus. Church-related universities which impose strict dorm regulations for females make it inconvenient and hazardous (e.g., suspension) to live together.

Although parents, peers, and university tolerance influence living together during college, these same factors combine to effect a radical drop after graduation. Living together is easy to conceal in a large university community; not so when Mel must move to another city for his job. Does Betsy go with him? What does she tell her parents? What does Mel tell his parents? Already they experience more pressure to marry since continued parental concealment is more difficult.

Peer support for living together is also scattered after college. Living in apartments near a university where several friends also live together is different from living in an apartment outside the university community. The life style of "do your own thing" and the social support from peers is replaced by neighbors who are more likely to follow society's norms, who may be tolerant, but who are also frequently married.

The uncaring university posture toward student (old role) attitude and behavior is slowly replaced by employers who project new expectations on the college graduate (new role). As a student, anything goes; as an employee, it is frequently a new set of directions. A college female majoring in education can student-teach while living with her boyfriend. After graduation her living-together behavior is more suspect. Even though the principal may be personally indifferent to her lifestyle, his job is dependent on what parents think of the teachers he hires. Since parents of youngsters are likely to be less approving of the teacher living with her boyfriend than the university community, the female will experience increased pressure (expressed through her employer) to marry.

When the random sample of Pennsylvania State University students were asked for their post-college living arrangement preferences, marriage was the most frequently selected alternative with cohabitation a close second and communal living a poor sixth choice (Peterman, Ridley, and Anderson, 1974). Maxine Edwards (1973) asked 768 students from seven colleges representing five regions of the United States to identify the life style most meaningful to them. Seventy percent noted that they believed the traditional monogamous marriage is the most fulfilling type of man-woman relationship. Carlfred Broderick (1972) observed that college students who say that marriage is obsolete, to be replaced by living together, are caught between institutions. They no longer feel controlled by their parents (family of orientation), yet they have not begun their own family (family of procreation). Although most couples who live together do use some form of contraception, a pregnancy is reacted to in terms of abortion or marriage. Society is willing to allow its youth to live together under the guise of improving intelligent mate selection. It is probably not willing to sanction a generation of babies whose parents are bound together by companionship feelings only.

Marriage meets a number of society's goals. It is the only unit that effectively stabilizes adult personalities (at least, most of the time) and replenishes the society with socialized members. Hence, living together is probably not a true alternative to marriage: most couples cannot live together and have children without a legal (marriage license) and social (wedding ceremony) commitment. Rather, living together may represent a pattern that is crystallizing as a stage in the life cycle of some young adults (Arafat and Yorburg, 1973).

LIVING TOGETHER—SOME CONSIDERATIONS

Before moving your clothes and personal belongings to your partner's apartment, you might consider clarifying certain issues in regard to marriage, parents, children, sex, living arrangements, finances, and legalities.

Marriage

Expectations about marriage should be clarified. Is it a "let's see" arrangement or is marriage the expected result? It is important that you not assume your partner intends to marry you if he does not. Even though you may choose to marry your partner or choose that your partner not leave you, your partner *may* leave you and marriage may *not* occur. If this happens, it will be important that you define yourself in positive terms rather than feel as though you have been used. In other words, you should decide to live together with someone in an unmarried state on the basis of the positive consequences which you anticipate will occur whether or not you get married.

Parents

Should you tell your respective parents that you are living together? Jackson and Jackson (1973) contend that, all things considered, honesty may be the best policy. They suggest that if your parents are going to disapprove of your relationship, it may be better for them to label you as immoral rather than immoral and dishonest. On the other hand, they suggest a careful consideration of your parents' background and their predicted response to the knowledge that you are living together with someone. If considerable grief and sorrow will result from the knowledge that you are living together, an attempt to delay that information and possibly avoid their sorrow may have the most positive consequence. However, be prepared to put up with the hassle of guarding your relationship, surprise visits, and phone calls.

Children

Do either or both of you want children while you are living together? If not, who is responsible for contraception? Are there any complications about which contraception, if any, is to be used? For example, one male said, "It's her responsibility to keep from getting pregnant." However, his fiancee's medical history obviated the use of the pill, she could not retain an IUD, and a diaphragm was considered "unacceptable."

Sex

Does living together imply that you will have intercourse? Occasionally partners decide to live together for economic reasons and choose to confine their sexual relations to partners other than the person with whom they are living. Will you and your partner have intercourse? If so, does this imply sexual exclusivity? Will you have intercourse only with each other or may one partner or both have sex outside of the relationship? It is less important what your answers are to these questions than that the expectations of your relationship be clarified.

Living Arrangements

How many will live together? Although you may assume that only the two of you will share an apartment or house, is this the case? One study reported that 60 percent of the cohabiting experiences involved living in a situation that involved several parties—roommates, friends, and others (Peterman, Ridley, and Anderson, 1974). After one coed moved in with her boyfriend, she discovered that his two roommates would continue to live there also.

Finances and Legalities

If you decide to live together *instead* of getting married, *not* as a prelude to marriage, there are financial and legal drawbacks to consider. For example, depending on whether your state recognizes common-law marriage, you and your partner may not be able to file a joint income tax return (as married people can) and thereby save money. (The Internal Revenue Service follows individual state's views on common-law marriage).

Second, health insurance policies taken out by the male will not cover the female unless she is his legal wife. Most hospitalization policies carry maternity benefits for delivery, pre- and postnatal care, but only the legal wife can benefit.

The legal drawbacks include no community property, no alimony, no legitimization of children, and no inheritance. Although these may be of little concern during college, after graduation the consequences may be more real. For example, suppose Kathy and Walt graduate and move from the college community. Walt works and Kathy stays home to care for their young child—Timmy. After two years, Kathy complains because Walt stays at work later and later. He reacts by telling her to leave him alone. An argument ensues. Walt moves out and in with another girl (the girl at work).

While Kathy is out of town, Walt moves the stereo, tapes and record albums, furniture, and bamboo drapes to his new apartment. Kathy goes to see a lawyer who informs her that since she is not legally married to Walt there is:

1. No community property. She cannot get the furniture and stereo back because they belong to Walt. If she were his wife, she would have a legal right to half of everything they owned.
2. No alimony. Although Kathy can force Walt to pay child support (if she can prove Timmy is his child), she will have to move from her apartment or face eviction since the child-support payments are not sufficient to pay the rent.
3. No legitimization of Timmy. Kathy's child is illegitimate, by definition. Although Kathy may not mind, Timmy's school peers may scornfully ask, "Where's your daddy?"
4. No inheritance rights. If Walt dies without a will, his legal wife would be entitled to inherit ⅓ to ½ of what he owned. The law makes no provision for inheritance by girlfriends. In addition, although most males carry life insurance policies, which pay significant sums upon the death of the insured, Kathy will not benefit. Since Walt subsequently married, his new wife and children by her will benefit.

Although Kathy's response to Walt's moving out was deep depression, Susan's story is different. She and Bill had been living together for a year-and-a-half when he left. Susan reacted calmly. "O.K.; I don't want a man living with me unless he wants to. I don't need him. I can make it emotionally and financially on my own."

Even though the tone of these remarks sounds like Susan is bitter and vindictive, she is not. She sees life as a changing process with no guarantees on anything—least of all, people. Her life motif is: "Give and love all you can—it will come back to you. If somebody takes advantage of you or uses you, that's his problem." Susan moved to another city with her daughter and is now attending graduate school. She loves her work and is "involved" in another relationship. She is happy.

SUMMARY

Living together is unique. Although it does not have the legal and social support of marriage, it is based more on companionship than a one-night stand, and allows for more realistic exposure to the partner than dating. The increased incidence of living together among college students can be attributed to supportive peer attitudes, tolerance by the University Community, availability of "the pill," and absence of parental knowledge. Living together after graduation (away from the university) may decrease as peer support is scattered, conservative employers replace tolerant university faculty, and secrecy from parents becomes more difficult.

Most college students who have lived together report that the experience was a meaningful one. About one-third of these couples break up and another third get married. There is little evidence to indicate that couples who live together are substantially different from those who do not.

Before choosing to live together, issues regarding marriage, parents, children, sex, and living arrangements should be discussed. Discussing these issues beforehand may prevent later misunderstandings. Where the decision is made to live together as a substitute for marriage, the legal and social drawbacks may be severe.

It seems certain that living together will continue to increase on the college campus. Unfortunately longitudinal studies on the evaluation of the experience are not available. Until such studies are made, a fundamental question remains: What are the long-term consequences of living together for the individual and for the relationship?

STUDY QUESTIONS

1. List several terms which refer to some form of heterosexual experience in which the unmarried partners share food and bed at a place each partner defines as their residence.

2. Discuss how living together is unlike marriage, unlike one-night sex, and unlike dating.

3. Living together is increasing. Why?

4. What are the three different commitment patterns of couples who live together?

5. Describe a typical campus living-together arrangement in terms of how the couple began to live together, where they live together, how the domestic chores are divided, and the sources of income.
6. How are parents a major problem for couples who live together?
7. Compare couples who live together with those who don't.
8. Evaluate the statement, "Living together is harmful."
9. Discuss why living together usually does not continue after graduation and after moving to a non-academic setting.
10. What issues should be considered before deciding to live together?

BIBLIOGRAPHY

ARAFAT, I. S. and YORBURG, B. On living together without marriage. *Journal of Sex Research,* 1973, **9**, 21–29.

BERGER, M. E. Trial marriage: Harnessing the trend constructively. *The Family Coordinator,* 1971, **20**, 38–43.

BRODERICK, C. B. *et al. Marriage: For and against.* New York: Hart Publishing Company, 1972, p. 263.

COFFIN, P. The young unmarrieds. In *Intimate life styles,* edited by Joann Delora and Jack Delora. Los Angeles: Goodyear Publishing Company, 1972.

COLE, C. L. Abstract of research. In *Cohabitation Research Newsletter,* Issue Number 1, September, 1972, p. 3. Used by permission.

CROAKE, J., KELLER, J. F. and CATLIN, N. *Unmarrieds living together: It's not all gravy.* Dubuque, Iowa: Kendall/Hunt Publishing Co., 1974.

EDWARDS, M. P. College students' perception of experimental life styles. Master's thesis. Oklahoma State University, 1972. Used by permission.

HENZE, L. F. and HUDSON, J. W. Personal and family characteristics of non-cohabiting and cohabiting college students. Used by permission. Unpublished (1974).

HOBART, C. Trial marriage among students: A study of attitudes and experience. Unpublished paper. University of Alberta, 1972. Used by permission.

HUDSON, J. and HENZE, L. F. Abstract of research. In *Cohabitation Research Newsletter,* Issue Number 1, September, 1972, p. 5. Used by permission.

JACKSON, T. and JACKSON, J. *Living together: A guide for unmarried couples.* Unpublished manuscript, 1973. Used by permission.

JOHNSON, M. P. Courtship and commitment: A study of cohabitation on a university campus. Master's thesis. University of Iowa, Iowa City, 1969. Used by permission.

———. Commitment: A conceptual structure and empirical application. *Sociological Quarterly,* 1973, **14**, 395–406. Used by permission.

LAUTENSCHLAGER, S. Y. A descriptive study of consensual union among college students. Master's thesis. California State University, Northridge, 1972. Used by permission.

LEDERER, W. J. and JACKSON, D. D. *The mirages of marriage.* New York: W. W. Norton, 1968.

LINDSEY, B. B. The companionate marriage. *Redbook,* March, 1927.

LYNESS, J. L., LIPETZ, M. E. and DAVIS, K. E. Living together: An alternative to marriage. *Journal of Marriage and the Family,* 1972, **34**, 305–11.

MACKLIN, E. D. Heterosexual cohabitation among unmarried college students. *The Family Coordinator,* October, 1972, **21**, 463–72. Used by permission of the National Council on Family Relations and the author.

PETERMAN, D. J., RIDLEY, C. A. and ANDERSON, S. M. A comparison of cohabiting and non-cohabiting college students. *Journal of Marriage and the Family,* 1974, **36**, 344–54. Used by permission of the authors.

REISS, I. L. *The social context of premarital permissiveness.* New York: Holt, Rinehart, and Winston, 1967.

ROGERS, C. R. *Becoming partners: Marriage and its alternatives.* New York: Dell Publishing Company, 1972.

RUE, J. From Betty Liddick's Practicing marriage without a license. In *Marriage Means Encounter,* ed. George Roleder. Dubuque, Iowa, Wm. C. Brown Company, Publishers, 1973, p. 174.

SCANZONI, J. H. *Sexual bargaining: Power politics in the American marriage.* Englewood Cliffs, N.J.: Prentice-Hall, Inc., 1972.

SIMMONS, J. L. and WINOGRAD, B. Sex and the "hang loose" ethic. In *American marriage: A changing scene,* edited by Frank Cox. Dubuque, Iowa, Wm. C. Brown Co., 1972, 194–204.

WELLS, T. and CHRISTIE, L. S. Living together: An alternative to marriage. *Futurist,* 1970, **4**, 50–51.

WHITEHURST, R. N. Living together unmarried: Some trends and speculations. In Michael J. Sporakowski and Mary Hicks (Eds.), *Families, Individuals, and Marriage.* Dubuque, Iowa: Kendall/Hunt Publishing Co., 1974.

6

Stay Single?

In tomorrow's world, being single will be no crime.

ALVIN TOFFLER [1]

I can't imagine promising my whole lifetime away.
I might want to get married now but how about
next year?

A COLLEGE STUDENT

The single life is becoming a valid alternative to marriage. In 1971, there were 15.5 million single males and 12.5 million single females (Moran, 1971). The number of single women is increasing. In 1960, 28 percent of the females aged 20 to 24 were single. In 1970, the number jumped to 36 percent (Bird, 1972). Although some are unmarried [2] by default (reasons include lack of suitable partners from the "right" social class, race, ethnic, religious, educational and age group; responsibility for parents; physical handicaps; personality inadequacies; and career involvement), many want to be single.[3] Even though most will eventually marry, the sense of urgency

[1] Alvin Toffler. *Future shock*. Copyright © 1971 by Random House, Inc. Used with permission.
[2] The terms "single" and "unmarried" are used interchangeably in this chapter. Both terms are used in the sense of never married.
[3] Books on how to be happy though single (Hillis, Marjorie. *Live alone and like it*. New York: The Bobbs-Merrill, Co., 1936; Glover, Janice. *Sense and sensibility for single women*. Garden City, New York: Doubleday and Co., 1963; Van

to do so is being replaced by relaxed enjoyment in being single. In this chapter, we review the single life style, social pressure to marry, research on single adults, and issues to consider if you choose to remain single.

THE SINGLE LIFE—BOTH SIDES

Freedom

For the young, economically independent, urban, college-educated, the single life style has a captivating fascination. This life style allows for continued change, geographic mobility, travel, a wider range of interpersonal relationships, and avoidance of a potentially devastating emotional and financial disaster—divorce.

Married life has a predictable pattern. People meet, marry, move to suburbia, have babies, rear them, and go into debt to pay college expenses. Whereas conventional marriage is usually presented as a package with directions on the front describing in detail the life ahead, the single life often bounces from night to night and from week-end to week-end. Some singles experience continuous opportunity for spontaneous excitement.

The single life not only offers a life style that may be more spontaneous than marriage, it involves genuine geographic mobility. Although one couple in four move every five years, three in four do not (Hobart, 1963). Economic responsibilities take precedence over the desire for continuous mobility. Once a spouse gets a steady job, he tends to keep it for fear of not being able to find another. The fear of loss of income is highly aversive and often confines the couple to one geographic location.

Children, too, often have a geographic settling influence on the married couple. The husband and wife, now parents, may consider the potentially negative effects of "uprooting the children" in adolescence when they have developed strong personal relationships with their peers. One aging father said, "We made a mistake moving at a time when our son's peer relationships had become stable. Once those relationships were destroyed, he was hesitant to become involved with friends again." The single person usually experiences none of these concerns. Rather, he is free to discover the delights of living in different places.

Remaining single may involve not only an unpredictable life style

Evera, J. *How to be happy while single.* New York: J. B. Lippincott, Co., 1948) inadvertently suggest an apologetic attitude for the unmarried female as evident in the following quotes: "Five out of ten people who are single can't help it and at least three of the others are irritatingly selfish" (Hillis, 1936, p. 15); "While you may not be to blame for your husbandless state, you could be at fault for fussing about it" (Glover, 1963, p. 6); "To explain her single state, a girl should say, 'I'm not married—now'" (Van Evera, 1948, p. 15).

and geographic mobility, but more freedom to travel. This advantage differs from geographic mobility in that it involves movement from one place to another for pleasure. The Golden Gate Bridge in San Francisco, Broadway plays in New York, the French Quarter in New Orleans, and Underground Atlanta offer an array of new experiences singles can enjoy. This freedom to travel may be unavailable to the married couple shackled with expenses and children.

The single person may also experience positive relationships with several different people throughout his life. Somehow, our culture teaches us that one relationship that lasts for fifty years is better than twenty-five relationships that last for two years. This is a value judgment yet to be empirically demonstrated. It seems ironic that from the age of eight through eighteen we are encouraged to date as many people as possible and to "play the field," but once a marital commitment is made, we are expected to experience all interpersonal satisfaction with primarily one person and have only secondary, superficial relationships with others. The freedom to experience an unlimited number of relationships is probably the most impressive advantage of remaining single.

Freedom for the single female now includes sexual freedom. Not only can she escape from the moral restraints of living in her home town, but also her concern over pregnancy is obviated with the pill and IUD. "She is less concerned with being chaste than being chased—and caught—perhaps often before she marries" (*Time* Essay, "The Pleasures and Pain of the Single Life").

The single person will also avoid the potential emotionally and financially devastating experience of divorce. The single male will suffer neither the anguish of being separated from his children by law nor the penalty of paying money to a woman whom he has learned to hate. Similarly, the female will not be burdened with the upbringing of children he has spawned on the fifty dollars a month stipend for each child which he grudgingly and belatedly pays.

In addition to these reasons for remaining unmarried, one attractive, single, Ph.D. female said, "I don't want to give up my name or credit rating. Marriage would force me to do both." In essence, the person who chooses to remain single values something else more than marriage (e.g., independence, credit rating, or travel).

Loneliness

The price of freedom may be unwanted loneliness. The single person, who does not live with someone, is continually living between events or persons. Although movie, dinner, and other dates often include staying overnight, there is the inevitable return to the apartment—empty as before. A dog, cat, or bird may dispel feelings of loneliness, but two-way conversation is necessary to give meaning to reality (Berger and Kellner, 1972). Happiness is not happiness if it is not shared (Wright, 1973).

The Concord in the Catskill mountains of New York is one of several hotels offering week-ends for singles. An advertisement for one of their week-end specials offers an insight into the lonely side of the single life. The caption reads, "This may be your last single week-end."

The desire for privacy and freedom is like selecting food in a cafeteria—it is easy to get more than you want. The desire to be alone is sometimes instantly transformed into an unwanted dictum—you will be alone. As one stewardess said, "There are times I feel I will go crazy if I have to be alone again in my apartment."

Free or Lonely—In Perspective

The proverbial belief that the grass is greener on the other side haunts both the married and the single person. Each may muse that life would be different (and better) if only it were possible to transcend the present state. In reality, neither is the blissful haven presumed by the other. The sharing of emotional companionship assumed of the married by the single is a nightmare to some married couples. Likewise, the presumed ecstasy of freedom, characteristic of the single life, may carry with it feelings of meaninglessness and unbearable loneliness for the single person.

PRESSURE TO MARRY

Our society is biased toward marriage. We assume that by age thirty everyone should be married. In this section, we analyze why society is concerned about marriage and how it pressures the unsuspecting single into marriage.

Pressure—Why?

The regulation of sexual behavior, role sharing for mutual economic maintenance, stabilization of adult personality, man's need for structure, and protection for and socialization of children are standard societal reasons for marriage. Although our society is, perhaps, willing to accept that physiological, economic, and psychological needs can be met outside of marriage, it is less willing to approve of children being reared in an unmarried environment.

Babies are the basis of societal pressure toward marriage. It is their care, protection, and socialization that accounts for the social concern for marriage. "Marriage is rooted in the family, not the family in marriage" was observed by Westermarck (1922).

The insistence by society that mothers should also be wives will diminish as two new trends continue: (1) voluntary childlessness, and (2) adoption by single adults. The traditional reasons for having children are disappearing. Our society is in little danger of dying out if every female does not reproduce. The population explosion which threatens human existence has obviated the cultural encouragement to have more children. Large families are more frequently seen as unnecessary and unwise.

In addition to society no longer needing babies for replacement (of dying members), an increasing number of females believe that having a baby is unecessary for their fulfillment and identity. One by-product of the women's liberation movement has been to put motherhood in perspective. It is only one of several alternatives open to the female. She may define herself in terms of her career involvement, values, and goals which need not be in reference to a husband or children.

The positive effect of children on personal and marital happiness has also become suspect. One mother of two pre-school children said "The best time of the day is when the kids are in bed." In regard to marriage, some evidence indicates that children reduce happiness rather than create it (Blood and Wolfe, 1960; Dyer, 1963; Hurley and Palonen, 1967). Although other studies (Luckey, 1966; Hobbs, 1965) conflict with these findings, Hicks and Platt (1970) reviewed the literature on the effect of children on marital happiness and concluded, "Perhaps the single most surprising finding to emerge from research is that children tend to detract from, rather than contribute to marital happiness." In effect, children are not essential for societal replacement, personal identity, or happiness (personal or marital).

In addition to increased voluntary childlessness, continued adoption by single adults will further separate having children and being married: Single-parent adoptions have been made in Los Angeles, New York, Washington, D. C., Chicago, and other major cities. In some instances, the single adoptive parents have been men. At this time, only children termed "hard to adopt" (those over two years of age, with handicaps, or of mixed race) are available to a single person (Kadushin, 1970).

Adoption agencies are hesitant to allow single adults to adopt normal children. The implication is that the single-parent family may be more likely to encourage "pathology" in the developing child. Although research is divided on the issue, the conclusion seems to be that internal dynamics rather than family structure *per se* is the important variable related to later pathology (Rodman and Grams, 1967). On this basis, more single adults will be allowed to adopt children.[4]

Marriage will diminish in importance when children are considered a separate issue from it. Not only are children unnecessary to fulfill social and personal needs (of some people), single parents may prove extremely effective in socializing the young. (Carol Klein's book, *The Single Parent Experience* (1973) may serve as a guide for single parenthood.) Until these trends gather momentum, however, pressure toward marriage will continue.

Pressure—How?

To encourage everyone to marry, society uses stereotypes and primary relationships. The unmarried are victims of outrageous stereotyping. Their single status is attributed to sexual inadequacies (frigidity and impotence), homosexual tendencies, unbridled selfishness, and an inability to relate to others on other than a superficial basis. These negative stereotypes are often embedded in the interaction between the single adult, his parents, and friends. It is through these primary relationships that society achieves maximum social control.

Although parents generally do not want their son or daughter to marry "too early" (before completion of the training period), with each successive year in school, the intensity and depth of the questions increases: "Are you dating anyone?", "Who are you going with?", "When are you going to get married?", and "What's wrong with you?".

Friends may exert a more subtle pressure through marrying and then asking you about your plans. The question, "What do you plan to do when you graduate?" often has the connotation "When are you getting married?"

RESEARCH ON THE NEVER-MARRIED

The stereotypes of "single" and "married" obscure the reality of the individual person. It is assumed that the single female is lonely, bitter, and

[4] Adoption agencies look for certain characteristics of prospective single parents: (1) Close ties with the extended family. (2) The availability of male relatives—uncles, brothers, nephews—permit the possibility of intimate contact for identification with father surrogates. (3) The availability of money to prevent the adoptive mother from always doubling as a wage earner during the dependent years of the child. (4) Considerable attention is given to the issue of sexual identification of the single applicant and the nature of the relationship with the opposite sex. Why is the person divorced, single, etc.? (5) The health of the single applicant is important. If the "parent" gets sick, who can care for the child? (6) The motivation of the single person seeking a child is also assessed. For example, does the applicant act out of an aching loneliness, out of the need to have and control a source of love and affectional response? (Kadushin, 1970).

unhappy with her "fate," while the married woman is happy and fulfilled in her role of wife and mother. A comparison of the single female and the single male is also at the expense of the female. Our culture projects an image of her waiting by the phone in her empty apartment while the debonair male is enjoying a candlelight dinner with one of "his" attractive girls (ownership of a harem is implied). When the bachelor is compared to the married male, the latter is described by the proverbial ball and chain. In this section, we shatter these stereotypes by reviewing the research on the single and married adult.

Single Female vs. Married Female

In general, the negative stereotype of the unhappy single female lacks empirical support (Srole, *et al.,* 1962; Baker, 1968; United States Public Health Service, 1970). To assess the relationship between mental health and marriage among females, Srole and his colleagues interviewed 256 single and 437 married women aged 20–59. The results indicated that the two groups reflected similar "mental health profiles." For example, the ability to adapt to stress, the ease of social interaction, and a sense of social belonging were characteristic of the single as well as the married females (Srole, *et al.,* 1962).

In another study, Baker (1968) wanted to ascertain if marriage and motherhood were essential to feminine fulfillment. He administered the California Test of Personality, which assesses personal and social adjustment, to 38 never-married women and 38 married mothers. In addition to comparing similar age groups (mean of 56 for never-married; mean of 48 for married), he attempted to match the samples for educational, community, religious, and occupational background. He concluded that the never-marrieds were no different from the marrieds in their personal and social adjustment. Said Baker:

> The never-married subjects in this investigation expressed no feelings of frustration, no sense of not being a "whole person" as a consequence of being unmarried. Their sense of personal worth comes not from their biological function as a female but from their social function as a human being, from what they perceive as a creative contribution to their significant society (Baker, 1968, p. 479).

In support of these conclusions, the United States Public Health Service [5] observed fewer symptoms of distress (nervousness, insomnia,

---

[5] Survey conducted in 1960–1962 on probability sample of 7710 persons selected to represent 111 million adults in United States civilian, non-institutionalized populations aged 18–79. Full reference can be found in bibliography under U.S. Department of Health, Education, and Welfare.

nightmares, headaches, and so forth) in single women as compared with married women.

Do single females differ from married females in regard to physical attractiveness, personality characteristics, and adolescent romantic involvements? Klemer (1954) compared 30 single and 30 married, college-educated women of similar ages (30–39), living in an urban community. Although the single females were, on the average, equally as attractive as the married females, more extreme personality characteristics were observed among the single women. For example, they tended to be either more shy or more aggressive. (It is possible that a stable marital relationship provides an atmosphere in which shy behavior disappears. The married female may feel free to be who she is, whereas the single person may exhibit more shy behavior until emotionally secure in a relationship. Aggressive behavior may be a function of a more defensive posture against the negative stereotype of the single person.)

In regard to earlier heterosexual involvement, the married women had had more dates, love affairs, and romances between the ages of 16 and 25 than the single women. This finding may indicate that the married female had more social skills than the single female. Those social skills which increased heterosexual interaction also increased the probability that a romantic relationship geared toward marriage would develop.

In essence, when the single woman is compared with the married woman, her mental health differences are slight. The negative stereotype of the single woman has no empirical base. Rather, some evidence suggests that the single female is happier and better adjusted than her married sister.

Single Female vs. Single Male

Cultural stereotypes of the unhappy, lonely, listless, single female and the jubilant bachelor are shattered when the life states of the two are empirically compared. Single males present a bleak picture. Knupfer, Clark, and Room (1966) asked 42 older single women and 36 older single men about their feelings of depression, loneliness, and happiness. Although a third of both groups reported that they experienced feelings of depression "often or sometimes," single men were much more likely to feel lonely and unhappy.[6] Other studies (Gurin, *et al.,* 1957; Bradburn, 1963; and Srole, *et al.,* 1962) demonstrated that single females report more happiness and fewer adjustment problems than single males.

Two explanations suggest why single males make a comparatively poor adjustment to life (Srole, *et al.,* 1962). First, single males may

---

[6] Thirty-nine percent of the single men reported loneliness compared to 29 percent of the single women. Nineteen percent of the single men reported feelings of unhappiness compared to 7 percent of the women.

represent a rejected lot. While the female may be single because she was not chosen, it is more possible that the single male was rejected. He has the cultural option of asking a female to marry him. Continued rejection may spring from physical or personality defects (physical: extremely "ugly" or handicapped; personality: unusual behavior such as always talking about self or paranoid). These defects, psychological or physical, make adjustment to life difficult for the single male, and the rejection by females may also result in a very poor self-concept. All maladjustment in the single male cannot be accounted for by the rejection hypothesis since many single males choose to remain single and are without obvious personal, social, or physical defects.

A second theory suggests that single males have fewer "meaningful relationships" than single females. In a study by Knupfer, et al. (1966), single men were more isolated, had fewer friends and experienced fewer interpersonal relationships.[7] These data suggest that while relationship needs of single women may be met through friends and the extended family, the single male does not cultivate these relationships to the same extent and may feel that he "shouldn't bother" others when he gets lonely. As one bachelor said, "When I feel lonely, I don't feel right about phoning someone and intruding on their life. I just get me a beer and watch TV."

Some males remain single by choice. In addition to the attractiveness of the single life, some males may have negative attitudes toward marriage. By remaining single, they escape the unhappy experience of marriage. Knupfer, et al. (1966), compared the parental marriages of single males and females. He observed that a significantly greater proportion of males evaluated their parents' marriage as unhappy.[8] However, in contrast to this finding, Rallings (1964) compared 100 single and 100 married males on the basis of family background variables. Although he found that the single males tended to come from families in which alcohol was a family problem (this same phenomenon was found in Knupfer's 1966 study), he concluded that there was a "striking similarity" between the two groups.

Single Male vs. Married Male

The single and married males represent opposite extremes of mental health. When compared on the basis of their subjective feelings of happiness, the single males are about twice as likely to report low levels of happiness

[7] Percent living alone—70% of the single men, 53% of the single women. Percent close to no one—24% of the single men, 17% of the single women. Percent who kept problems to self—64% of the single men, 51% of the single women.

[8] Sample size of single males = 46; of single females = 53; 59% of the single males rated marriage of parents as unhappy; 38% of the single females rated marriage of parents as unhappy.

(Gurin, *et al.,* 1960; Bradburn, 1963; Knupfer, *et al.,* 1966; Srole, *et al.,* 1962) as the married males. Single males also report more depression, feelings of loneliness, and anxiety (Knupfer, *et al.,* 1966).

Explanations for these findings parallel those suggested for the discrepancy between single males and single females. Although some males are single by choice, the bulk may be so by default. Since males in the United States traditionally marry down in age, social characteristics, and education, those left after the pairing has taken place are the inferior men and the superior women. The single male, rejected because of physical or behavioral deficits, may internalize a negative self-image which leads to further withdrawal from people.

These data and hypotheses should be considered cautiously. Some males (handsome and ugly; educated and uneducated), capable of intense emotional relationships, choose to remain single. Their selection of the single life does not spring from rejection, the burden of parental responsibilities, negative attitudes toward marriage, or homosexuality but rather from a rational choice to enjoy life unmarried.

STAYING SINGLE—SOME CONSIDERATIONS

The thesis of this chapter has been that remaining single is a valid alternative to marriage. But just as some people adjust poorly to marriage, others may have a similar reaction to a prolonged unmarried state. In this section, we review the conditions which may maximize enjoyment and adjustment in the single life.

Social Relationships

As noted earlier, the maintenance by the single adult of close interpersonal relationships with parents, siblings, and friends was associated with a more positive adjustment among singles. Since humans are social beings, their happiness is related to their relationships with others. Although they need not be married (legally committed), meaningful companionship with someone, some of the time, is necessary.

This suggests the importance of maintaining primary group ties (parents and siblings) or developing meaningful relationships with those who share similar values, goals, and life styles. Where the social skills are lacking for developing close relationships, involvement in social-skills seminars may be extremely valuable. The single life is a potentially lonely life. However, meaningful interpersonal relationships can be developed and maintained outside of marriage.

Economic Independence

Whereas the lack of involvement in meaningful interpersonal relationships is the critical problem of adjustment for the single male, that of the single female is money. She must have the capacity and opportunity to be economically self-supporting. Otherwise, she will be dependent on her parents who may attempt to restrict her movement and activity. Parents, who say "Live with us and save money," often mean, "Live with us and remain our little girl."

Economic independence is essential not only to break from parental controls, but also to insure the continued choice of remaining single. If sufficient money is limited there is the gnawing thought, "Why be single and work when I can be married and have a man support me?" Marriage has traditionally been explained as an exchange of money for sex. A female who chooses to remain single must be economically self-sufficient.

Social and Psychological Independence

Aside from economic independence, single females must be socially and psychologically autonomous. A female choosing the single life must recognize that a relationship with a man is not the exclusive source of social identity or emotional satisfaction (Adams, 1972). Her philosophy must permit her to enjoy men without feeling subjected to or controlled by them.

If she does not establish an identity apart from a male or the role of a wife, the probabilities are low that the single life will be satisfactory. The studies by Baker (1968) and Ellis (1952) of single females demonstrate the importance of their achieving social and psychological identities through career involvement.

The male can more easily achieve social and psychological autonomy since his identity is less tied to a wife and children. The career of the male can legitimately give him the status and recognition which, traditionally, the female has achieved through marriage.

Sexual Independence

Since marital sex is the only culturally approved form of sexual behavior, the single adult must satisfy his sexual desires outside the traditional pattern. Although masturbation may serve to cover extended time periods between relationships, heterosexual intercourse with another unmarried may be the most desirable alternative. The choice of the single life coupled with the decision to engage in unmarried intercourse necessitates a positive attitude toward self and sex. For example, a single person who chooses to maintain a healthy self-concept and who also chooses to have intercourse with no hint of marriage, must define the experience and himself (herself) in positive terms. This is in contrast to the single person who has intercourse, yet feels guilty if no marital commitment is involved.

SUMMARY

Few people choose to remain single. Of those who do, females seem to make a better life adjustment than males. The single male represents a gloomy existence when compared to single females and married males. Rejection and avoidance of close interpersonal relationships have been suggested as the primary difficulties of single life for the male. Although the research reflects a dejected single male, individual cases indicate a positive attitude and adjustment toward being single.

The single adult has some unique concerns. Whereas the male should exercise particular care to establish meaningful relationships, the single female must focus on being economically, socially, and psychologically independent. Although unmarried sex is deviant sex (has weak social approval), each person must develop a sex life consistent with his own values and self-concept. Remaining single *is* a choice. For some, the single life may be more rewarding than any other life alternative.

STUDY QUESTIONS

1. Discuss several advantages of remaining single.

2. What is the potential price of freedom for the single person?

3. What is the basis of societal pressure for marriage? Under what conditions might this pressure diminish?

4. In what ways, if any, have you experienced pressure to marry?

5. Compare the single female and the married female, the single female and the single male, and the single male and the married male in terms of general mental health and social relationships.

6. What issues should the male and female consider before deciding to remain single?

BIBLIOGRAPHY

ADAMS, M. The single woman in today's society: A reappraisal. In *The woman's movement: Social and psychological perspectives,* edited by Helen Wortis and Clara Rabinowitz. New York: John Wiley and Sons, Inc., 1972, pp. 89–101.

BAKER, L. G. The personal and social adjustment of the never-married woman. *Journal of Marriage and the Family*, 1968, **30**, 473–79.

BERGER, P. and KELLNER, H. Marriage and the construction of reality. In *Woman in a man-made world*, edited by Nona Glazer-Malbin and Helen Youngelson Waehrer. Chicago: Rand McNally and Company, 1972, pp. 174–82.

BIRD, C. Essay on marriage. In *Marriage: For and against.* New York: Hart Publishing Co., 1972, pp. 169–86.

BLOOD, R. O. and WOLFE, D. M. *Husband and wives: The dynamics of married living.* Glencoe, Illinois: The Free Press, 1960.

BRADBURN, N. M. *In pursuit of happiness.* Chicago: National Opinion Research Center, 1963.

DYER, E. D. Parenthood as crisis: A re-study. *Marriage and Family Living*, 1963, **25**, 196–201.

ELLIS, E. Social psychological correlates of upward social mobility among unmarried career women. *American Sociological Review*, 1952, **17**, 558–63.

GLOVER, J. *Sense and sensibility for single women.* Garden City, New York: Doubleday and Co., 1963.

GURIN, G., VEROFF, J. and FELD, S. *Americans view their mental health.* New York: Basic Books, Inc., 1960.

HICKS, M. W. and PLATT, M. Marital happiness and stability: A review of the research in the sixties. In *A decade of family research and action*, edited by Carlfred B. Broderick. Minneapolis, Minn.: The National Council on Family Relations, 1970, 59–78.

HILLIS, M. *Live alone and like it.* New York: The Bobbs-Merrill Co., 1936.

HOBART, C. Commitment, value conflict and the future of the American family. *Journal of Marriage and the Family*, 1963, **25**, 405–12.

HOBBS, D. F. Parenthood as crisis: A third study. *Journal of Marriage and the Family*, 1965, **27**, 367–72.

HURLEY, J. R. and PALONEN, D. P. Marital satisfaction and child density among university parents. *Journal of Marriage and the Family*, 1967, **29**, 483–84.

KADUSHIN, A. Single-parent adoptions: An overview and some relevant research. *Social Service Review*, 1970, **44**, 263–74.

KLEIN, C. *The single parent experience.* New York: Walker, 1973.

KLEMER, R. H. Factors of personality and experience which differentiate single from married women. *Journal of Marriage and Family Living*, 1954, **16**, 41–44.

KNUPFER, G., CLARK, W. and ROOM, R. The mental health of the unmarried. *The American Journal of Psychiatry*, 1966, **122**, 841–51.

LUCKEY, E. B. Number of years married as related to personality perception and marital satisfaction. *Journal of Marriage and the Family,* 1966, **28,** 44–48.

MORAN, R. The singles of the seventies. In *Intimate life styles,* edited by Joann S. Delora and Jack R. Delora. Goodyear Publishing Co., 1972, p. 338.

RALLINGS, W. M. A comparative study of the family situations of married and never-married males. Unpublished Ph.D. dissertation, Florida State University, 1964.

RODMAN, H. and GRAMS, P. Juvenile delinquency and the family: A review and discussion. In task force report: *Juvenile delinquency and youth crime,* by the President's Commission on Law Enforcement and Administration of Justice. Washington, D.C.: Government Printing Office, 1967, pp. 188–221.

SROLE, L., LANGER, T. S., MICHAEL, S. T., OPLER, M. K., RENNIE, T. A. C. *Mental health in the metropolis: The midtown Manhattan study.* New York: McGraw-Hill Book Co., Inc., 1962.

TOFFLER, A. *Future shock.* Copyright © 1971 by Random House, Inc. Used by permission.

United States Department of Health, Education and Welfare. Public Health Service. Selected Symptoms of Psychological Distress. National Center for Health Statistics, Series 11, #37. Vital and Health Statistics—August, 1970.

VAN EVERA, J. *How to be happy while single.* New York: J. B. Lippincott and Co., 1948.

WESTERMARCK, E. A. *The history of human marriage.* 3 vols. New York: Allerton Book Co., 1922.

WRIGHT, J. Department of Sociology, Tulane University, New Orleans, Louisiana, 1973. Personal communication, used by permission.

III

WHY?

If there were not two of us, the question of why would never occur.

B. F. SKINNER [1]

Traditionally, people have given certain reasons for marriage. "We are in love" often serves to satisfy ourselves and others as an appropriate answer to the question, "Why are you getting married?" Our answers are probably more a function of saying whatever is necessary to stop the questioning rather than an accurate revelation of our feelings and/or reasons for our behavior. For example, a senior coed publicly said "I'm in love," but privately said, "If I don't marry him now, there may be no one else." Since escaping loneliness was not an acceptable reason for marrying, she glibly told her parents and friends she was in love.

It is difficult to explain precisely why one individual marries another. Explanations are so influenced by individual, partner, parent, and peer variables that no single answer seems accurate. Some of these explanations

---

[1] Richard I. Evans. *B. F. Skinner, The Man and His Ideas.* Copyright © 1969 by Richard I. Evans. Published by E. P. Dutton & Co., Inc. and used with their permission.

(love, sex, and other reasons) for marriage are discussed in Part III.

There are, perhaps, two acceptable reasons for getting married: (1) Your belief that marriage with this person will offer more productive short- and long-term consequences than (a) living together; (b) remaining single; or (c) becoming involved with someone else. And (2) The productive long- and short-term consequences of the marriage imply greater happiness for you *and your partner* than you or your partner could achieve alone or with someone else. Embedded in each of these criteria is the suggestion that you are not marrying solely for any temporary reason (pregnancy, rebound, escape, and so on) but, rather, because of predicted long-term positive consequences.

7

Love

I married for love and got a little money along with it.

ROSE FITZGERALD KENNEDY [1]

"Because we are in love" is the reason most frequently given for the decision to marry. The feelings experienced by two people involved in an intimate interpersonal relationship often propel them toward marriage. They may feel guilty if they are in love and do not talk of marriage or a life together. Likewise, marriage without love may seem equally strange.

This chapter reviews the nature of love, its origins and elements. It encourages you to assess your ideas about love and compare them with those of your partner and other college students.

NATURE OF LOVE

Love is a difficult concept to understand. The refrain of an old song aptly expresses the difficulty of getting a firm grip on the experience of love:

[1] Rose Kennedy in interview on WPBR, Palm Beach, Florida, and quoted in *Newsweek*, January 29, 1973. Reprinted by permission.

For love is such a mystery,
I cannot find it out,
For when I think I'm best resolved,
I then am most in doubt.[2]

One researcher noted "The word love denotes a world that is illimitable and I shall never see the whole of it" (Benoit, 1955). And Morgan (1964) wrote "It is in order here to disavow any intention of expounding the 'real meaning' or 'essence' of love. There is no such thing."

Although love will be discussed in terms of an attitude composed of certain elements and as a feeling ranging on a continuum from romanticism to realism, the specific meaning of love has been defined in different ways by different peoples at different times. For example, the Buddhists conceived of two types of love—an "unfortunate" kind of love (self love), and a "good" kind of love (creative spiritual attainment). The latter concept was defined in terms of a "love of detachment," not in the sense of withdrawal from the emotional concerns of others but in the sense of gladly accepting them as they are and not requiring them to be different from their present selves as the price of friendly affection. To a Buddhist, the "best" love was one in which you accept others as they are without requiring them to be like you (Burtt, 1957).

Three concepts of love introduced by the Greeks and reflected in the New Testament are: *phileo, agape,* and *eros. Phileo* is friendship love which covers many relationships. For example, the love you experience for your brother or sister (*philadelphia*) may be quite different from the love you have for people in general (*philanthropia*).

Agape means a love of self-sacrifice that is spontaneous and unmotivated (Nygren, 1953). This type of love is altruistic and requires nothing in return.

Eros is a type of selfish love which seeks to get from another what is valuable to the "taker." Intercourse without affection is a good example of *eros*. Each partner may be using the other for self-gratification without true concern for the other person.

LOVE IS LEARNED

The development of love feelings may be explained from different points of view. We will first consider love from a learning perspective.

[2] From *Happy Marriage* by John A. O'Brien. Copyright © 1956 by John A. O'Brien. Reprinted by permission of Doubleday & Company, Inc.

Love feelings are not "built in" but come from learned social responses, for example, a smile, a touch, a laugh. Most of the things that make us feel good are incorporated into our cultural system of dating and court-ship; we treat the other person very courteously, smile a lot, try to be pleasant, avoid saying offensive things, dress to look attractve, use best manners, and perhaps dine on food and enjoy entertainment that takes us beyond our budget. More importantly, all of these pleasurable features appear against a background of escalating physical stimulation or sexual excitement. Indeed, we have a social interaction in which one's dating partner is paired with the widest possible range of pleasurable sensations and activities (Bartz and Rasor, 1972, used by permission).

Consider this explanation of love in your dating relationship. Think about someone you just met. It is not possible for this person to elicit love feelings in you unless you have already shared a number of pleasurable experiences (e.g., eating together, seeing movies together, talking together). The "love at first sight" experience is the result of seeing someone whose features (eyes, face, body type) have already been paired with love feelings. For example, it would be difficult for you to fall romantically in love with someone three times your age. This love possibility with an elderly person is reduced because you have not experienced love (romantic) feelings with someone that age nor have you been taught to expect love feelings. The experience of love requires a cultural readiness.

The behaviors which cause love feelings must be reinforced to be maintained. This implies that during a developing relationship, couples have a high frequency of reinforcing each other for appropriate behavior. This results in the partner continuing the desired behavior which results in the continuation of love feelings. If you want your partner to continue to engage in behavior which you define as desirable, you must reinforce or reward that behavior.

Love dies when partners spend little time together and stop sharing activities that are mutually enjoyable (movies, dances, eating out, or what-ever). As a test for this phenomenon, identify an unhappy couple you know and specify how much time they spend together engaging in enjoy-able behavior. Contrast this with a couple you define as being in love and observe the amount of time they spend in mutually enjoyable activities. Love can be created or destroyed by pairing or failing to pair the partner with pleasurable activities over time.

The death of love also results from failure on the part of both partners to reinforce appropriate behavior in each other. For example, smiling, caressing, complimenting, spending time together, and helping with the baby are behaviors in marriage that may not be reinforced. When these behaviors are no longer reinforced, they will stop. If your partner stops doing things that you like, your love feelings will disappear. It is important that you reinforce your partner for positive behavior (so that the behavior will continue) to insure that there is a continued basis for your love feelings.

In summary, love is a function of sharing pleasurable activities with each other over time, reinforcing your partner, and being reinforced by your partner for appropriate behavior. When partners stop spending time with each other in pleasurable, mutual activities and stop reinforcing each other for appropriate behavior, love dies.

OTHER THEORIES OF LOVE

Aside from understanding love from a learning perspective, sexual, social, psychic, and theological explanations have also been suggested.

Sexual

The sexual origin of love was suggested by Freud, who believed that love was a feeling of tenderness and affection which resulted from blocked biological, organic, sexual desires and wants. He referred to love as "aim-inhibited sex." He noted that "Love with an inhibited aim was originally full sensual love and, in man's unconscious mind, is still so" (Freud, 1960). In other words, the love you experience for your partner is a function of your sexual desire for your partner which is not allowed to achieve full expression outside of marriage. As the permissiveness-with-affection pre-marital sexual standard (intercourse within a context of love) continues to increase among college students, Freud's theory will continue to be viewed with serious skepticism.

Social

In contrast to the sexual explanation, another theory considered love as a positive instinctive feeling seeking response from others and com-panionship with them. Love was seen as social rather than sexual. "The specific origin of love, in time, is at the moment the infant recognizes the existence of others," noted Suttie (1952).

Psychic

Another theorist said that love was neither sexual nor social, but psychic. Reik (1949) wrote, "The origin of love belongs to the ego-drives."

By this he meant that love sprang from a state of dissatisfaction with one's self and was a vain urge to reach one's "ego-ideal." He believed that love was a projection of one's ideal image of himself on another person. For example, suppose you do not have dark blue eyes but wish you did. According to Reik's thesis, you would have a tendency to fall in love with someone who had blue eyes. For another example, suppose that you are a shy person who values the qualities of assertiveness. Consistent with Reik's theory, it would be easy for you to fall in love with someone who took control of situations and who was assertive. In other words, you would love in someone else the qualities which you lacked.

Theological

Borrowing from Plato and emphasizing a theological explanation, Tillich (1960) conceived of love as a drive towards the unity of the separated. He believed that "Reunion presupposes separation of that which belongs essentially together. Therefore, love cannot be described as the union of the strange but the union of the estranged" (Tillich, 1960). Tillich made reference to the legend that man and woman were originally housed in one body. However, because God lost favor with his first creation, he split his creation in half—man and woman. Since that separation, man has continually been looking for woman and vice versa, each to complement the other and to regain their togetherness. Tillich believed that when you seek a mate for marriage, you are trying to identify that portion of you which was once together but which is now separated.

In addition to the learning, sexual, social, psychic, and theological explanations of love, other researchers and writers have provided variations of these theories. Waller (1938) referred to love as "the anesthetic which renders the amputation of our cherished habits painless." By this he meant that individuals were willing to give up the advantages of being single (freedom, irresponsibility, and mobility) in exchange for the feeling of committed love. In contrast, Russell (1929) believed that love was the "principal means of escaping from the loneliness which afflicts most men and women throughout the greater part of their lives."

Fromm's (1963) concept of love is similar to Russell's in that he sees love as a means of overcoming the "separateness" of man and of quelling the anxiety of his loneliness. Man is considered by Fromm, Russell, and Suttie (1952) to be incomplete without the experience of love.

Just as there is no definitive answer as to the nature of love, there is no single universally accepted theoretical explanation for its origin. In essence, the meanings of love are as divergent as its theoretical bases.

ELEMENTS OF LOVE

A helpful way to discuss love is in terms of the various elements of which it is composed. For example, although we might all disagree on what love is or is not, we might find some agreement if we consider that love consists of certain elements in various combinations. The notion that love consists of various elements has been observed by Kierkegaard (1949). He said that different factors comprising love may be combined in many different ways in the individual. Earlier, Shand (1914) noted that, "Love is not a simple emotion but a sentiment compounded of many emotions." These authors suggest that love can only be discussed in terms of its elements.

There are, perhaps, four central elements of love: physical, intellectual, emotional, and social. Consider each of these elements in regard to heterosexual love. The love you experience for your partner is partly physical (sexual). You may enjoy touching, holding, rubbing, kissing, stroking, and the like.

The intellectual element of love consists of sharing thoughts with your partner. You may have experienced the ecstasy of getting into your partner's head and liking what you found. To understand and to feel that you are understood by another is often involved in the development of love.

Love may also have an emotional element. Spinoza, the philosopher, said, "We want things not because we have reasons for them; we have reasons for them because we want them." He was saying that we are ruled primarily by emotion; we use logic to justify our behavior.

Love also involves a social element. It is difficult to love someone independent of other social relationships. One of the reasons love is a possibility with a particular person is because he (she) "fits in well" with at least some of your social relationships. It is easier to love someone if your friends, parents, and siblings approve. Love occurs within a social context.

Although love consists of various elements, most people expect and enjoy its behavioral expression. This implies that if you love your partner you will demonstrate your love by engaging in behavior which your partner defines as desirable. Conversely, if your partner loves you, he or she will engage in behavior which you define as desirable. Partners who love each other do things for each other. (This does not imply justification for "proving love," e.g. through having intercourse. If your partner loves you, he will not pressure you to do something inconsistent with your values.) Love not expressed behaviorally is not love. If your partner loves you he will spend much of his leisure time with you and will do things for you.

YOUR ATTITUDE TOWARD LOVE

What do you believe about love? What does your partner believe about love? Two copies of "The Love Attitude Inventory" [3] (Table 7-1) are presented to help assess your respective ideas about love. If you are interested in these perspectives, complete copy 1 of the inventory and ask your partner to complete copy 2 before reading further.

The Love Attitude Inventory is designed to measure your tendency to view love in a romantic versus a conjugal (or realistic) way. Since 1 (strongly agree) is the most romantic response and 5 (strongly disagree) is the most conjugal or realistic response, the lower your total score, the greater your tendency to view love in a romantic way (30 is the lowest possible score). The higher your total score, the greater your tendency to be conjugal or realistic in your attitude toward love (150 is the highest possible score). If you scored below 90 (the mid-point between 30 and 150), you have a more romantic attitude toward love than if you had scored above 90. Your partner's score will suggest his basic perspective on love. Romantic or realistic views of love should be considered as different *ways* of viewing love rather than "good" or "bad" kinds of love.

Before explaining the significance of some of the individual items in Table 7-1, it may be helpful to discuss the characteristics of romantic and conjugal love.

ROMANTIC LOVE

These are some of the characteristics of rȯmantic love: *Cultural heritage*—differences in custom, tradition, class, and religion are of small importance in selecting a marriage partner as compared with love. *True love comes but once*—there is only one person with whom you can fall in love. *Mysticism*—love is strange and incomprehensible. *Love at first sight. Cardiac-respiratory love*—emphasis upon excited love, thrills, and palpitations of the heart. *Complete involvement and exclusivity*—lovers are completely absorbed with each other; outside entanglements are unthinkable and admission of ambivalence is tantamount to denial of love. *Daydreaming*—indulgence in reverie and inattention. *Jealousy*—believed to vary directly with seriousness of love. *Love alone*—seen as criterion for marriage. *Urgency*—dogma of "gather ye rosebuds while you may." *True love is eternal* (Gross, 1944).

[3] "The Love Attitude Inventory" and portions of the *Guide to Accompany the Love Attitude Inventory*, by D. H. Knox, Jr., copyright © 1971 by Family Life Publications, Inc., Saluda, North Carolina, are used by permission.

TABLE 7-1   *The Love Attitude Inventory, Copy 1*

Directions: Please read each sentence carefully and circle the number which you believe best represents your opinion. Be sure to respond to all statements.

1. Strongly agree (definitely yes)
2. Mildly agree (I believe so)
3. Undecided (not sure)
4. Mildly disagree (probably not)
5. Strongly disagree (definitely not)

	SA	MA	U	MD	SD
1. Love doesn't make sense. It just is.	1	2	3	4	5
2. When you fall head-over-heels-in-love, it's sure to be the real thing.	1	2	3	4	5
3. To be in love with someone you would like to marry but can't, is a tragedy.	1	2	3	4	5
4. When love hits, you know it.	1	2	3	4	5
5. Common interests are really unimportant; as long as each of you is truly in love, you will adjust.	1	2	3	4	5
6. It doesn't matter if you marry after you have known your partner for only a short time as long as you know you are in love.	1	2	3	4	5
7. If you are going to love a person, you will "know" after a short time.	1	2	3	4	5
8. As long as two people love each other, the religious differences they have really do not matter.	1	2	3	4	5
9. You can love someone even though you do not like any of that person's friends.	1	2	3	4	5
10. When you are in love, you are usually in a daze.	1	2	3	4	5
11. Love at first sight is often the deepest and most enduring type of love.	1	2	3	4	5
12. When you are in love, it really does not matter what your partner does since you will love him anyway.	1	2	3	4	5
13. As long as you really love a person, you will be able to solve the problems you have with that person.	1	2	3	4	5
14. Usually there are only one or two people in the world whom you could really love and be happy with.	1	2	3	4	5
15. Regardless of other factors, if you truly love another person, that is enough to marry that person.	1	2	3	4	5
16. It is necessary to be in love with the one you marry to be happy.	1	2	3	4	5

TABLE 7-1 *(cont.)*

1. Strongly agree (definitely yes)
2. Mildly agree (I believe so)
3. Undecided (not sure)
4. Mildly disagree (probably not)
5. Strongly disagree (definitely not)

	SA	MA	U	MD	SD
17. Love is more of a feeling than a relationship.	1	2	3	4	5
18. People should not get married unless they are in love.	1	2	3	4	5
19. Most people love truly only once during their lives.	1	2	3	4	5
20. Somewhere there is an ideal mate for most people.	1	2	3	4	5
21. In most cases, you will "know it" when you meet the right one.	1	2	3	4	5
22. Jealousy usually varies directly with love; that is, the more you are in love, the greater your tendency to become jealous.	1	2	3	4	5
23. When you are in love, you do things because of what you feel rather than what you think.	1	2	3	4	5
24. Love is best described as an exciting, rather than a calm, thing.	1	2	3	4	5
25. Most divorces probably result from falling out of love rather than a failing to adjust.	1	2	3	4	5
26. When you are in love, your judgment is usually not too clear.	1	2	3	4	5
27. Love often comes but once in a lifetime.	1	2	3	4	5
28. Love is often a violent and uncontrollable emotion.	1	2	3	4	5
29. Differences in social class and religion are of small importance as compared with love in selecting a marriage partner.	1	2	3	4	5
30. No matter what anyone says, love cannot be understood.	1	2	3	4	5

Please add the numbers you have circled and write the total in the following space: _____.

TABLE 7-1 The Love Attitude Inventory, Copy 2

Directions: Please read each sentence carefully and circle the number which you believe best represents your opinion. Be sure to respond to all statements.

1. Strongly agree (definitely yes)
2. Mildly agree (I believe so)
3. Undecided (not sure)
4. Mildly disagree (probably not)
5. Strongly disagree (definitely not)

	SA	MA	U	MD	SD
1. Love doesn't make sense. It just is.	1	2	3	4	5
2. When you fall head-over-heels-in-love, it's sure to be the real thing.	1	2	3	4	5
3. To be in love with someone you would like to marry but can't, is a tragedy.	1	2	3	4	5
4. When love hits, you know it.	1	2	3	4	5
5. Common interests are really unimportant; as long as each of you is truly in love, you will adjust.	1	2	3	4	5
6. It doesn't matter if you marry after you have known your partner for only a short time as long as you know you are in love.	1	2	3	4	5
7. If you are going to love a person, you will "know" after a short time.	1	2	3	4	5
8. As long as two people love each other, the religious differences they have really do not matter.	1	2	3	4	5
9. You can love someone even though you do not like any of that person's friends.	1	2	3	4	5
10. When you are in love, you are usually in a daze.	1	2	3	4	5
11. Love at first sight is often the deepest and most enduring type of love.	1	2	3	4	5
12. When you are in love, it really does not matter what your partner does since you will love him anyway.	1	2	3	4	5
13. As long as you really love a person, you will be able to solve the problems you have with that person.	1	2	3	4	5
14. Usually there are only one or two people in the world whom you could really love and be happy with.	1	2	3	4	5
15. Regardless of other factors, if you truly love another person, that is enough to marry that person.	1	2	3	4	5
16. It is necessary to be in love with the one you marry to be happy.	1	2	3	4	5

TABLE 7-1 *(cont.)*

1. Strongly agree (definitely yes)
2. Mildly agree (I believe so)
3. Undecided (not sure)
4. Mildly disagree (probably not)
5. Strongly disagree (definitely not)

	SA	MA	U	MD	SD
17. Love is more of a feeling than a relationship.	1	2	3	4	5
18. People should not get married unless they are in love.	1	2	3	4	5
19. Most people love truly only once during their lives.	1	2	3	4	5
20. Somewhere there is an ideal mate for most people.	1	2	3	4	5
21. In most cases, you will "know it" when you meet the right one.	1	2	3	4	5
22. Jealousy usually varies directly with love; that is, the more you are in love, the greater your tendency to become jealous.	1	2	3	4	5
23. When you are in love, you do things because of what you feel rather than what you think.	1	2	3	4	5
24. Love is best described as an exciting, rather than a calm, thing.	1	2	3	4	5
25. Most divorces probably result from falling out of love rather than a failing to adjust.	1	2	3	4	5
26. When you are in love, your judgment is usually not too clear.	1	2	3	4	5
27. Love often comes but once in a lifetime.	1	2	3	4	5
28. Love is often a violent and uncontrollable emotion.	1	2	3	4	5
29. Differences in social class and religion are of small importance as compared with love in selecting a marriage partner.	1	2	3	4	5
30. No matter what anyone says, love cannot be understood.	1	2	3	4	5

Please add the numbers you have circled and write the total in the following space: _____.

The "Love Attitude Inventory" and portions of the *Guide to Accompany the Love Attitude Inventory,* by D. H. Knox, Jr., copyright © 1971 by Family Life Publications, Inc., Saluda, North Carolina, are used by permission.

CONJUGAL (OR REALISTIC) LOVE

In regard to conjugal or realistic love, Goode stated, "The antithesis of romantic love is conjugal love—the love between settled, domestic people" (Goode, 1959). The opposite of the characteristics of romantic love are viewed as characteristics of conjugal love. In addition, specific writers have indicated a conjugal perspective in their definitions of love:

When the satisfaction or the security of another person becomes as significant to one as is one's own security, then the state of love exists (Sullivan, 1947).

Love is the passionate and abiding desire on the part of two or more people to produce together the conditions under which each can be and spontaneously express his real self; to produce together an intellectual soil and an emotional climate in which each can flourish, far superior to what either could achieve alone (Magoun, 1948).

Love is that intense feeling of two people for each other which involves bodily, emotional, and intellectual identification; which is of such a nature as to cause each willingly to forego his personality demands and aspirations in favor of the other; which gains its satisfaction through creating a personal and social identity in those involved (Koos, 1953).

The love of a person implies not the possession of that person, but the affirmation of that person. It means granting him, gladly, the full right to his unique humanhood (Overstreet, 1949).

In essence, romantic love is a love of longing, the condition or readiness to look upon another in a favorable light all of the time. It is the anticipation of fulfillment forever which holds no hint of doubt or flaw. On the other hand, conjugal or realistic love is a love of acceptance, the condition or readiness to look upon another in a favorable light most of the time with the understanding that the light may occasionally dim and flicker.

Discussion of Specific Items in Table 7–1

The way you marked specific items in The Love Attitude Inventory (Table 7–1) indicates your attitude toward love. For example, if you circled a low number (1 or 2) for items 1 and 30, you believe that love is a wonderful abstraction, beyond scientific scrutiny. On the other hand, if you circled a 4 or 5, you believe that love makes a great deal of sense since its presence or absence, as well as the conditions under which it exists, can be identified. You recall that love is composed of specific elements (physical, intellectual, emotional, and social) which vary in intensity relative to the perception of the love object.

Items 2, 4, 7, 11, and 21 make reference to the idea of love at first sight. Since this does occur, it is inaccurate to label it as a foolish belief. If you agreed with these statements, you are probably still "in love" with the person you "fell in love with at first sight." Time is yet to tell if love at first sight for you is the most enduring type of love. If you have experienced the dissipation of an initial whirlwind love affair, you probably circled a 4 or 5. Generally, love is based on a regard for the total personality which cannot be "known" at first glance. Infatuation can develop immediately and is based on a predominant physical and sexual concern. Unless couples spend a great deal of time together, it is difficult for love to develop. However, infatuation may become love.

A romantic response to items 3, 16, and 25 assumes that love and marriage must always occur together for maximum happiness. If you circled a 1 or 2, you may have had the experience of being in love with someone at a time when marriage was not practical. Romeo and Juliet in Shakespeare's play are the prototypes of frustrated love. If you mildly or strongly disagreed with any or all of these statements, you believe that a strong, unfrustrated love can be experienced between people who are not married, just as a married couple may be very happy, but not in love. Likewise, partners who get divorced may love each other, but not be happy living together.

Items 5, 8, 9, 13, 15, and 29 share the theme that "love conquers all." Similar friends, religions, and interests are not prerequisites for love. If you circled a 1 or 2, you believe that people with different backgrounds, attitudes, and interests have the same, perhaps greater, probability of falling in love and staying in love than those with similar characteristics. However, if you mildly or strongly disagreed with those items, you believe that love grows best in a soil of similarity. Burgess and Cottrell (1939) in *Predicting Success or Failure in Marriage* noted that better adjustment is often characteristic of couples who have similar backgrounds (religion, friends, and social class). This does not imply that people of different orientations do not meet, establish happy love relationships, marry, and continue to experience satisfaction in their relationships. Rather, they may have to work harder to build a common base.

Strong or mild agreement with item 6 indicates a belief that it is appropriate for a couple to meet and marry within a few weeks, so long as they are in love. This position assumes that love alone is the sole criterion for marriage. Research on the positive relationship between length of acquaintance and adjustment in marriage was presented in Chapter Four. Partners who have known each other for at least a year prior to marriage are more likely to be better adjusted and to remain married than those who have been acquainted for shorter periods of time. Agreement with item 6 has been scientifically researched, and such research indicates the necessity for caution of meeting and immediately marrying on the basis of "love" alone.

Items 14, 19, 20, and 27 reflect the romantic belief that "true" love occurs only once in a person's life. If you strongly or mildly agree with these statements, you are probably still dating your first love and do not contemplate a change, or you have never been in love and are waiting for that special moment. The conjugal response of disagreement with these items is buttressed by the fact that many widowed and divorced people meet others, establish love relationships with them, marry, and define themselves as happy. Although it may seem that, at the time you break up, you can never love another person as much as you did your partner, empirical evidence demonstrates that you can.

Jealousy and Love

Many students have demonstrated an interest in item 22 which is about jealousy and love. Margaret Mead noted that jealousy was the result of loss of status. If Bob chooses to spend most of his leisure time with Carol rather than Mary, Carol gains in status and Mary loses. As a result, Mary may become jealous of Carol, who outranks her in Bob's value system.

If Carol is convinced of Bob's love, she will not be jealous of his spending time with others, since the threat of loss of love and status does not exist. Her status with Bob is secure. On the other hand, if Mary is unsure of Bob's love, she will be jealous of Carol and others since they are a threat to her.

A romantic attitude toward jealousy insists that it is a sign of love. It is also assumed (from a romantic perspective) that where jealousy does not exist, neither does love. On the other hand, the conjugal attitude toward jealousy is that it occurs in an unstable, insecure relationship. Consider your own love relationship relative to your feelings of security and jealousy.

LOVE ATTITUDES OF COLLEGE STUDENTS

When the Love Attitude Inventory was administered to 100 male and 100 female, single college students (Knox and Sporakowski, 1968), two significant relationships were found. The first was between attitude toward love and sex of the respondents. The data indicated that the females tended to be more realistic (or conjugal) in their attitude toward love than did the males. Conversely, the males viewed love more romantically than the females. The mean (average) score for the females was 98.89; for males, 94.45. It should be understood that the females were not realistic but *more* realistic than the males, and that the males were not romantic but *more* romantic than the females. Both males and females tended to be more realistic than romantic since both males and females had a mean score above 90.

The findings that males are more romantic than females support the speculation by Merrill (1949) that "man, rather than woman, may be the romantic animal." In addition, Hobart's (1958) finding that females were less romantic than males was corroborated by the present data.

Clearly stated, the female may have a greater tendency to be more realistic in attitude toward her love partner for two reasons: (1) greater pressure from kinship group, and (2) greater dependency on her mate for security.

Pressure from kinship group. Since, traditionally, the unmarried female has been considered to be less acceptable to American society than the bachelor, she may experience greater pressure from her parents and close relatives to marry and to do so wisely. Since she is expected to marry and to remain married, she may have a greater tendency to select a mate whom she believes will "wear well" over the years. Hence, she may have a more realistic attitude.

The male may also be influenced by his kinship group, which transmits to him cultural prescriptions and admonitions against flippant mate selection. However, since the male is less restricted by our normative system, he may tend to be less cautious in his selection of a bride and—perhaps—more romantic.

Need for security. Since, traditionally, the female has been dependent on her husband for her subsistence, and because she has assumed his standard of living, she may have a greater need to be more pragmatic in her selection of a mate. She may select a male whom she deems capable of providing for her materially. The exception is the career female who has her own status and income.[4]

The second significant relationship found was between attitude toward love and class in school. The mean scores were as follows: freshmen, 88.24; sophomores, 93.89; juniors, 97.35; and seniors, 99.35. These data clearly

[4] It should be kept in mind that this study was conducted before the Women's Liberation Movement had made its impact on college coeds. Bernard (1970) suggests that 15 percent of today's college females do not define happiness and fulfillment in terms of marriage. Rather, these students are interested in personal growth and development which may or may not include marriage.

indicate that as an individual advances in college, his attitude toward love becomes more realistic. Freshmen are more romantic than sophomores, sophomores more romantic than juniors, and so on. Seniors are the most realistic students on campus. Possible explanations for this include: (1) increased dating experience, (2) mental maturity, and (3) increased seriousness of dating relationship.

Increased dating experience. As the college student dates many people over a period of years, his ability to perceive and evaluate accurately the element of love in his relationship with his dates may increase. By "element of love" is meant the proper placement of love within the context of the total interpersonal relationship. Initially, the freshman may perceive love as the only reason for dating—to experience the thrill of involvement. He may imagine things about his date since he does not know her. As a senior who has had many dates with different people over a period of years, he may realize that the girl he dates is a real person who usually will not conform to whatever preconceived image he may have of her. Consequently, he has learned to perceive love more realistically.

Mental maturity. Unlike the freshman, the senior has been exposed to material in the academic sphere which may have encouraged him to view life more realistically. Although the freshman may still believe that love is "like it happens in the movies," the senior will usually have a more realistic perception. In addition to a general increase in reality orientation, the upperclassman may have taken a marriage course specifically designed to correct prevalent heterosexual misconceptions.

Increased seriousness of dating relationship. As the senior year approaches, many students begin to select a date in terms of a future mate rather than for a "romantic evening." Consequently, the criterion shifts from: "Can he (or she) dance?" to "Does he (or she) have life goals, values, and ideas that are consistent with mine?"

SUMMARY

Societal reasons for marriage are of little concern to the bride and groom who say "We're in love." The fact that marriage functions to stabilize adult personalities and replenish the society with socialized members rarely occurs to newlyweds who have been socially programmed to explain their biggest commitment of time and energy on the basis of their emotions—love.

In this chapter, we have reviewed the nature, origins, and elements of love. Love is a difficult concept to understand. Its meaning changes depending on the observer, the observed, and the time of observation. Likewise, the theoretical explanations for the origin of love vary from a blocked sex drive (Freud), to God splitting a unisex person (Tillich). The most useful way to explain love seems to be through understanding how the feelings of love are learned. The elements of love are more universally accepted than the various theories. Most adults have experienced some or all of the emotional, physical, social, and intellectual elements of love.

The characteristics of romantic versus realistic love, as well as the Love Attitude Inventory, were presented to assist you in assessing your and your partner's ideas about love. Compare these perspectives with the love attitudes of other college students. In general, college males and freshmen are more romantic in their attitude toward love than college females and seniors.

The word "love" is often used to express the emotional importance of two people for each other. In our culture, it is the great motive for commitment. In the next chapter, we discuss the equally powerful force which attracts people to each other—sex.

STUDY QUESTIONS

1. What do most people say when asked about their motivation for marriage?
2. What is the basic nature of love?
3. Define and give an example of *phileo,* of *agape,* and of *eros.*
4. Explain the creation and death of love from a learning perspective.
5. Why are you not likely to experience "love at first sight" with someone three times your age?
6. How did Freud explain love? How is his explanation viewed today?
7. What is the social explanation for love?
8. How did Reik conceive of love?
9. Discuss the theological explanation of love suggested by Plato and Tillich.
10. How did Waller view love?
11. What are four major elements of love?
12. How did Sullivan define love?
13. Distinguish between romantic and conjugal love.
14. Discuss two reasons why females may be more realistic in their attitude toward love than males.
15. Discuss three reasons why college seniors may be more realistic toward love than college freshmen.

BIBLIOGRAPHY

BARTZ, W. R. and RASOR, R. A. Why people fall in and out of romantic love. *Sexual Behavior,* December, 1972, 33–39. Quoted material reprinted by permission of the authors and publisher.

BEIGEL, H. G. Romantic love. *American Sociological Review,* 1951, **16,** 326–34.

BENOIT, H. *The many faces of love.* New York: Pantheon Books, 1955.

BERNARD, J. Women, marriage, and the future. *The Futurist,* 1970, 4.

BURGESS, E. W. and COTTRELL, L. S. *Predicting success or failure in marriage.* New York: Prentice-Hall, 1939.

BURTT, E. A. *A man seeks the divine.* New York: Harper and Brothers, 1957.

FREUD, S. *Group psychotherapy and analysis of the ego.* Translated by James Strachey. New York: Bantam Books, 1960.

FROMM, E. *The art of loving.* New York: Bantam Books, 1963.

GOODE, W. J. The theoretical importance of love. *American Soiological Review,* 1939, **24,** 38–41.

GROSS, I. A belief pattern scale for measuring attitudes toward romanticism. *American Sociological Review,* 1944, **9,** 963–72.

HOBART, C. W. The incidence of romanticism during courtship. *Social Forces,* 1958, **36,** 362–67.

JOHNSON, P. E. *Christian love.* New York: Abingdon-Cokesbury Press, 1951.

KIERKEGAARD, S. *Works of love.* Translated by D. F. Swenson and L. M. Swenson. New Jersey: Princeton University Press, 1949.

KNOX, D. H., JR. Attitudes toward love of high school seniors. *Adolescence,* 1970, **5,** 89–100.

———. Conceptions of love at three developmental levels. *The Family Coordinator,* 1970, **19,** 151–57.

———. Conceptions of love by married college students. *College Students Survey,* 1970, **4,** 28–30.

———. Discussion guide to accompany a love attitude inventory. Family Life Publications, Inc., Saluda, North Carolina, 1971.

KNOX, D. H., JR. and SPORAKOWSKI, M. J. Attitudes of college students toward love. *Journal of Marriage and the Family,* 1968, **30,** 638–42.

KOOS, E. L. *Marriage.* New York: Henry Holt, 1953.

KRICH, A. M. (ed.) *The anatomy of love.* New York: Dell Publishing, 1960.

MAGOUN, F. A. *Love and marriage.* New York: Harper, 1956.

MERRILL, F. E. *Courtship and marriage.* New York: Henry Holt, 1949.

MORGAN, D. N. *Love: Plato, the Bible and Freud.* Englewood Cliffs, New Jersey: Prentice-Hall, 1964.

NYGREN, A. *Agape and eros.* Philadelphia: Westminister Press, 1953.

O'BRIEN, J. *Happy marriage.* New York: Popular Library, 1957.

OGBURN, W. F. and NIMKOFF, M. F. *Technology and the changing family.* Boston, Massachusetts: Houghton-Mifflin, 1955.

OVERSTREET, H. A. *The mature mind.* New York: W. W. Norton, 1949.

REIK, T. *Of love and lust.* New York: Farrar, Straus, and Cudahy, 1949.

RUSSELL, B. *Marriage and morals.* New York: Horace Liveright, 1929.

SHAND, A. F. *The foundations of character.* London: Macmillan, 1914.

SULLIVAN, H. S. *Conceptions of modern psychiatry.* Washington, D. C.: William Alanson White Psychiatric Foundation, 1947.

SUTTIE, I. D. *The origins of love and hate.* New York: Julian Press, 1952.

TILLICH, P. *Love, power and justice.* New York: Oxford University Press, 1960.

WALLER, W. *The family.* New York: The Dryden Press, 1938.

8

Sex

*The notion is gaining ground among the young
unmarrieds, on the campus as elsewhere, that
unmarried sex is not at all identical with
"premarital" sex; that sex is its own justification,
without so much as a thought to marriage or any
expectation of marriage.*

L. LIPTON [1]

All social relations are maintained by the principle of reciprocity. This *quid
pro quo* (something for something) is evident in all interactions. Buying a
notebook at the campus bookstore involves an exchange of money. Helping
your roommate move to a new apartment implies your right to visit and
his indebtedness to help you in the future.

The decision to marry also involves reciprocal behavioral expectations.
Each partner attempts to strike the best bargain possible in terms of getting
the mate with the most desirable characteristics realizing what he (she),
in return, has to trade. Males typically offer the promise of being a "good
provider" in exchange for the rewards of the female's physical appearance,
social skills, and cooperativeness (Scanzoni, 1972).

Implied in the agreement to continue the premarital relationship is
actual or promised (as in the case of one who values virginity) sexual ex-

[1] L. Lipton. *The erotic revolution.* Los Angeles: Sherbourne Press, 1965. Reprinted by permission.

change. To withdraw sexual availability or the promise of it after marriage would threaten a core element of the relationship. Because of personal and societal expectations of marital sexual expression, the premarital relationship is likely to break if the partner consistently refuses to include sex as a negotiable item.

Desmond Morris (1971) described twelve stages in the development of a love relationship. The last nine stages involve physical contact (hand to hand, arm to shoulder, arm to waist, mouth to mouth, hand to head, hand to body, mouth to breast, hand to genitals and genitals to genitals). Sex is a vital part of the bargaining process during courtship. Although sex may occur without marriage, the reverse is rarely true. Marriage does not occur unless an agreement has been made regarding sex.

Males and females have been socialized to think and behave differently about sex. In this chapter, we review these respective meanings and behaviors. Although some evidence suggests that perspectives and behaviors of males and females are becoming more similar, until recently this has not been true.

There are tremendous variations in sexual attitudes and behaviors in the different social classes. Since most college students are middle class, the following discussion is specific to them. Lower and upper class sexual patterns, which in some cases are dramatically different, have not been emphasized.[2]

MALE SEXUALITY

Meaning of Sex and Love

Traditionally, males have been taught that masculinity is related to success in seduction. The more clothes a female takes off, the more masculinity he puts on. The traditional male has been socialized to think that "he isn't really a man" if he cannot persuade a female to have intercourse. This implies that the traditional male may not be emotionally involved with the female with whom he has intercourse. In one study, males were twice as likely as females to have intercourse with someone with whom they were not involved. The researcher concluded that male sexuality was inversely related to emotional commitment (Ehrmann, 1959).

In a more recent study of the first intercourse experience of 200 uni-

[2] For a discussion of sexual behavior in the noncollege world, see Chapter 9 of *Female and male: Dimensions of human sexuality* by Elaine C. Pierson and William V. D'Antonio (Philadelphia: J. B. Lippincott Company, 1974), and *Sexual conduct* by John H. Gagnon and William Simon (Chicago: Aldine Publishing Company, 1973).

versity students, 41 percent of the males had their first experience with a prostitute (11 percent), pickup, or casual date (30 percent). Almost one-third of these males never had intercourse again with their first partner (Eastman, 1972). The tendency for the male not to be involved with his sexual partner was also observed by Simon and Gagnon (1969). In their study, the males typically had intercourse with their first coital partners one to three times, while among females, it was ten times or more.

These figures suggest that male sexual behavior is homosocial—that males engage in sexual behavior with females in reference to their male friends; the emotional involvement with the female may be incidental (Gagnon and Simon, 1973). For example, to be accepted by his peers, a male may talk about his sexual experiences with a buxom coed. In so doing, he establishes his masculinity and his membership in the group. Emotional involvement with the female is unimportant since his male friends only ask, "Did you get any?" "Did you score?" or "Did you make out?"

Homosocial behavior is best illustrated by a male who told his roommate that he had had intercourse with the university homecoming queen. Since the roommate shouted in disbelief, a plan was devised so that he could verify the event. The scheme called for the roommate to hide in the trunk of the car while his friend had intercourse with the campus beauty in the back seat. The reader can imagine this proof of manhood being executed. Notice that the male is having intercourse in deference to his roommate, not the girl.

Masturbation

Within two years of puberty all but a few males have had orgasm, almost universally brought about by masturbation. The private and personal experience of masturbation for males leads to a capacity for a detached sexual orientation—the disassociation of love and sex mentioned above (Simon and Gagnon, 1969).

Males begin to masturbate around age 13 and do so about three times a week during their teens. The regularity of this orgasmic experience continues throughout life whether single, married, divorced, or separated (Saxton, 1972). On his wedding day, the average male has had over one thousand self-induced orgasms.

Kinsey noted that 96 percent of the college males in his sample had masturbated. This figure is in contrast to 87 percent of those who attended only grade school. Kinsey also observed that masturbation occurred most frequently among religiously inactive Protestants and least among Orthodox Jews and devout Roman Catholics (Kinsey, Pomeroy, and Martin, 1948).

In about three-fourths of males, masturbation is accompanied by fantasies or daydreams (Johnson, 1964). Gagnon and Simon (1973) refer to masturbation as the "thinking man's television." On his television screen he may imagine himself having intercourse with the "playmate of the month," the stripper he saw in a stag movie, or his girlfriend.

Reasons for masturbation vary. Although pleasure may be the predominant motive, reducing anxiety and avoiding intercourse are others. The college male who is anxious over grades, the relationship with his girl, his parents, or money may choose the alternative feelings of ecstacy and relaxation which can be induced instantly. Masturbation is quicker than intercourse since the latter usually entails a detailed procedure to get the partner ready for penetration.

A male may avoid intercourse for moral reasons or from fear of rejection. A small percentage of males consider intercourse before marriage immoral. Others lack the social skills necessary to seduce an unwilling female and after a series of rebuffs, avoid this rejection experience.

Petting

Petting (sexual contact which excludes intercourse) is the second most frequent form of sexual expression in the unmarried college male. Although petting often involves stimulating the partner manually or orally to climax, petting may also include "hunching," "humping," or "dry run." These words imply that the couple lie together with their clothes on or off and, with legs interwined, move rhythmically until ejaculation occurs. Those couples who choose to remain virgins until marriage often "hunch" to reduce their sexual anxiety while maintaining their values.

It is not unusual for couples who have petted to orgasm to discover that they are parents. This results when semen is deposited near the vagina at ejaculation, becomes lodged in the moist vaginal lips, and makes its way to fertilize an egg in the fallopian tubes. Penetration is not necessary for conception.

Intercourse

Kinsey (1948) observed that 67 percent of unmarried college males have had intercourse. Although figures cited in 1972 vary somewhat from Kinsey's data (Robinson, King, and Balswick, 1972; Broderick, 1972; and Mace, 1972), Saxton (1972) notes, "All published research since Kinsey agrees that male sexual behavior remains substantially unchanged in the 1950's and 1960's."

Unmarried college males who have intercourse subscribe to one of three sexual standards: the double standard, permissiveness without affection, and permissiveness with affection. The double standard holds that there is one standard for male sexual behavior (uninhibited sexual freedom) and another for the females they marry (sexual abstinence and/or fidelity).[3]

The permissiveness without affection standard suggests that premarital intercourse is permissible for both men and women regardless of the amount of affection or stability of the relationship. Sex is viewed as entertainment, and the primary law of morality is self-interest. The permissiveness without affection standard supports the position that neither man nor woman should be hindered in achieving his (her) basic desires, especially sexual pleasure, which is strongly affirmed as good in itself.

Permissiveness with affection suggests that "love makes it right." As long as two people are in love and feel close to each other emotionally, intercourse is justified. One researcher noted that premarital intercourse is moral if it strengthens the relationship of the couple and immoral if it weakens the relationship (Kirkendall, 1961). The permissiveness with affection standard is achieving increased acceptance among college males. A study of 3000 undergraduates on a California campus concluded, "Where it occurs, sexual intimacy seems to take place in the context of a relationship that is serious rather than casual" (Katz, 1968). Among Harvard college students, Vreeland (1972) observed that "the majority feel that sexual intercourse should be engaged in only by couples who feel they are in love."

Reiss (1972) summarized the trend: "Males in the 60's were beginning to feel that sex was best with someone they felt affection for; person-centered sex was much to be preferred to body-centered coitus. The male partners were shifting from the prostitute and the lower-class female to the girl next door."

Males who, traditionally, subscribed to the double standard and sought prostitutes or the easy campus lays, now tend to have intercourse with females within the context of an emotional relationship.

FEMALE SEXUALITY

When one male talks to another about feeling "horny or experiencing orgasm," each understands the other. When two females discuss similar sexual phenomena, great misunderstanding may occur. Kinsey noted that the most important finding of his research on female sexuality was that the concept of the "average" female is almost meaningless. He observed that the sexuality of each female is so unique that there is little chance that her own particular characteristics have ever existed before or will ever exist again (Kinsey, 1953).

---

[3] The double standard may be replaced by a single standard for males and females. "There appears to be a small group of young men who can truly maintain a single standard for themselves and the women they are involved with before and after marriage. And this may be the increasing pattern of the future" (Bell, 1972).

Meaning of Love and Sex

The degree of sexual involvement for females is directly related to the degree of psychological or personal involvement (Ehrmann, 1959). Traditionally, the female has been socialized to experience intercourse within a context of love. A study on first intercourse experiences by Eastman (1972) lends support to this thesis. He observed that 46 percent of the women indicated that they were in love and planning to marry the person with whom they had intercourse for the first time. This was in contrast to 11 percent of the males.

The problem of the female losing her virginity appears to be one of working out a means of avoiding labels of promiscuity (Whitehurst, 1973). Since the female has been traditionally socialized to experience sex within a context of love, the label "slut" or "whore" is extremely aversive. This is a major distinction in male-female sexuality. Whereas males may disregard the context of the relationship, females often demand personal involvement on the part of the male before they will have intercourse.

Although an emotional relationship may be desirable, some research suggests that college females are becoming more willing to have intercourse without it or a commitment for marriage. One study comparing the premarital sexual experience among coeds in 1958 and 1968 revealed that 23 percent of the coeds in 1968 were willing to have intercourse with males they were merely *dating* as opposed to 10 percent in 1958 (Bell and Chaskes, 1970). Another study noted that in 1970, 54 percent of the female sample said that a woman who had sexual intercourse with a number of men was immoral, whereas, in 1965, 91 percent of the females had agreed with that statement (Robinson, King, and Balswick, 1972). Whitehurst (1973) observed that a long-term relationship was desirable but not a necessary condition for the first intercourse experience of females. Two conclusions can be drawn from these studies: (1) although females may still prefer intercourse within the context of a relationship, they are less likely to demand a commitment for marriage as a prerequisite for intercourse; and (2) females today are more likely to value the experience of intercourse for itself than previously. Intercourse for sexual pleasure is now considered an option by the female.

Masturbation

Females usually learn about masturbation through self-exploration rather than peer instruction (Kinsey, 1953). Many females are appalled at the knowledge that some of their girlfriends actually feel themselves while those who enjoy masturbating regularly are appalled that their girlfriends do not enjoy regular masturbatory activities. This illustrates the great variability of experience and expectations of one female toward another to which Kinsey referred.

Clifford (1973) studied the masturbatory patterns of 100 undergraduate (random sample) women.[4] She investigated the following facets of female masturbation: incidence, frequency, technique, reasons, duration of masturbatory session, fantasy and frequency of climax. About half (49 percent) reported having masturbated. The frequency varied widely, with an average of one masturbatory session every two to four weeks.

Although great variations occurred, rubbing the fingers on and around the clitoris, mixing light and heavy pressure, with short and rhythmic strokes, while lying flat on the back was the most usual means of masturbating. Other procedures common among women who masturbated were: (1) squeezing the thighs together and (2) rubbing the general clitoral area on a smooth but hard edge, e.g. sitting down on the back of a chair.

Achieving pleasurable sensations was the most frequent motive given for masturbation among Clifford's sample. Release from tension and relieving loneliness were other prevalent reasons. Masturbation was most likely to occur when the female missed her partner (35 percent), after seeing sexy movies (34 percent), and when unable to sleep (34 percent).

The duration of a masturbatory session for these females ranged from 5 to 15 minutes, with some continuing for an hour or more. This sharply contrasts with the usual 3-minute duration of masturbation in the male.

The frequency of achieving climax was also different from the male. Whereas males are consistently able to achieve climax through masturbation, a significant proportion (26 percent) of these females who masturbated experienced a climax less than 90 percent of the time. Climax was usually achieved by stroking the area around the clitoris or the clitoris directly.

Although fantasy was reported to facilitate enjoyment for a majority of these females, it was not significant in inducing orgasm. Eighty-five percent said that they never needed fantasy or reading matter to achieve climax. When fantasy did occur, it most often consisted of kissing, petting, or having intercourse with a male with whom there was an emotional relationship or a physical attraction.

In regard to the relationship between masturbation and intercourse, Clifford observed:

> In the majority of cases, masturbation clearly acts as a substitute for intercourse. For 65 percent of those with both kinds of experience, an

[4] Clifford's findings generally support the Kinsey data collected over 20 years ago.

increase in intercourse resulted in a decrease in masturbation. As hetero-sexual behavior increased during college, masturbation faded out for a number of subjects. Many described masturbating only when their part-ners were away or between relationships and regarded masturbation under other circumstances as an act of disloyalty to their partners. At the same time, a sizable minority of these women regarded masturbation as an activity divorced from sexuality while satisfying other needs: for relaxa-tion, comfort, or diffuse enjoyment (Clifford, 1973).

Petting

Kinsey observed that petting was the most frequent form of sexual expression for females. He suggested that it is petting rather than the home, religious instruction, books, classes in biology, sociology or phi-losophy, or actual coitus that provides most females with their first real understanding of the heterosexual experience (Kinsey, 1953).

Kinsey also observed that petting before marriage was related to orgasmic capacity after marriage. Among the females who had never petted to the point of orgasm before marriage, 35 percent had never reached orgasm the first year of marriage. On the other hand, among those who had reached orgasm in at least some of their premarital petting, only 10 percent failed to reach it in the first year of marriage. Thus, petting is not only the first meaningful heterosexual experience for the female; it may increase the probability of orgasmic experience in marriage.

Intercourse

Several studies (Bell and Chaskes, 1970; Cannon and Long, 1971; Christensen and Gregg, 1970; Herr, 1970; Kaats and Davis, 1970; Mosher and Cross, 1971; Luckey and Nass, 1972) have documented an increased willingness of couples to engage in and to approve of premarital sexual relations. Zelnich and Kanter (1972) polled 4611 females ages 15 to 19 in 1971. Among 18-year-olds, 37 percent reported having had intercourse; among 19-year-olds, 45 percent had had intercourse.

The incidence of premarital intercourse is related to devoutness in religion, stage of involvement, and year in school (Schofield, 1965; Hatch, 1968; Clayton, 1969; Ehrmann, 1959; Reiss, 1967; Whitehurst, 1973). In general, college females who do not engage in intercourse before marriage tend to be religiously devout, uninvolved in an emotional rela-tionship with anyone, and freshmen in college. Females who engage in intercourse before marriage tend to be less religiously oriented, involved in a love relationship with a male, and in their senior year of college.

How do female college students react to losing their virginity? White-hurst (1973) interviewed 35 university females most of whom reported that the event was an emotionally gratifying experience. Some females mentioned negative consequences of the first intercourse in terms of a fear of being frigid or being labeled frigid, and pain or discomfort associated with intercourse. Some reported a concern for pregnancy or disease several days after the first intercourse. Although guilt was not expressed as a major consideration, there was an ever-present fear of being rejected or pushed aside because of the sexual relationship. Other research reports a less favorable reaction to first intercourse (Christensen and Gregg, 1970; Bell and Chaskes, 1970). About 30 percent of the respondents in these studies reported some feelings of regret and remorse that they had "gone too far."

Orgasm

Females who have not experienced an orgasm ask, "What is it like?" Women respond differently during sexual excitation. If a hundred women were to write their descriptions of an orgasmic experience, no two would describe the experience the same way. An orgasm consists of different feelings and sensations and may be highly subjective.

An orgasm is clinically defined as a pleasurable feeling which results from sexual excitation. The actual experience can be described in terms of cognitive and physiological processes. In regard to the cognitive processes, the female may label the experience as good, enjoyable, ecstatic, wonderful, and great. One woman described the experience as "champagne bubbles splashing through my veins." In addition to this positive labeling of the experience, many women experience a temporary loss of consciousness. For a brief moment, thought processes stop and it seems as though the person is dizzy with ecstasy. In addition to the positive labeling and loss of consciousness, some women express the experience as being one of warmth. One woman said, "I feel warm in my brain as well as in my vaginal area."

The physiological processes are easier to observe. The orgasmic experience is often accompanied by specific muscle contractions, rapid breathing, and a heart rate of 110 to 180 beats per minute. This peak experience is followed by some sweating in 30 to 40 percent of the cases.

The controversy over the clitoral versus the vaginal orgasm continues. Whereas Masters and Johnson emphatically state there are no physiological distinctions, 46 percent of the females in Clifford's study (1973) said there "is a difference." This difference is often described in terms of an emotional as opposed to a physiological distinction. The female subjectively experiences a climax (orgasm) during intercourse as qualitatively different from a climax induced through masturbation or manual manipulation. Regardless of how the climax is brought about, it is always associated with relaxation and comfort.

During the nineteenth century, women who experienced sexual satisfaction in marriage suffered extreme moral and scientific criticism. William Hammond, a surgeon-general of the United States asserted, that "nine-tenths of the time decent women feel not the slightest pleasure in intercourse." At the University of Basel, an eminent gynecologist named Fahling labeled sexual desire in young women as "pathological" (Hunt, 1959).

The modern theme of female sexuality suggests that orgasm is the woman's birthright. "It is necessary that she share the grandeur of the topmost heights with him—orgasm, the sexual climax—or else the enterprise becomes meaningless for both" (Davis, 1954).

NEW ANSWERS TO OLD QUESTIONS

Students enrolled in university marriage courses often ask specific questions about sexual behaviors which have not been covered in class or assigned readings. The following are examples of these questions and suggested answers.

Virginity

What's wrong with being a virgin?

Nothing. However, you should decide to be a virgin on the basis of predicted positive consequences. You should feel that you will have a better feeling about yourself, your partner, and your relationship if you remain a virgin. If your reason for virginity is because of your fear of sex, consider consulting a counselor. Fear of intercourse is a questionable reason for virginity since that fear may continue after marriage.

To assist individuals who choose to remain virgins, the American Virgin Liberation Front, which has offices in Philadelphia, Pennsylvania, has been formed to support those who practice virginity. Their dogma suggests that they are not against sex but want to establish the freedom of those persons who wish to refrain from sexual activity. Hence, the AVLF requests the right for individuals to maintain their self-respect and dignity if they choose to remain virgins.

Alternatives to Intercourse

How can I satisfy my partner and myself sexually without having intercourse?

This question is generated from the dilemma of the value of virginity competing with the desire for sexual release. The compromise which some couples have developed involves manually or orally manipulating the partner to orgasm. In this way, sexual anxiety is reduced and both maintain their labels as virgins.

Intercourse before Marriage

What percentage of engaged couples have intercourse before marriage?

Accurate statistics on premarital sexual behavior or any sexual behavior are not available. However, one study of 200 engaged college couples reported that 75 percent of the couples had had intercourse (Broderick, 1972).

Does intercourse before marriage decrease the chance of having a successful marriage?

There is no conclusive evidence at this time to suggest that having intercourse or not having intercourse before marriage results in a successful marriage. There is evidence which suggests that a premarital pregnancy has a negative effect on marital happiness (Stephens, 1968). If you decide to have intercourse before marriage, you should make another decision—about contraception. Do not allow one decision to count for two. In one study, 80 percent of the female respondents did not use any form of contraception the first time they had intercourse (Whitehurst, 1973). Do you want to have a baby at this time with this partner? If your answer is no, decide on and utilize an effective contraceptive. Pregnancy is the price of unprotected ecstasy.

Sex—How Much? How Soon?

What are some guidelines on sexual behavior the first few encounters?

There are no rules for the appropriateness of sexual behavior on dates. The absence of guidelines may be confusing. For example, if a male does not try to fondle the female during the first few encounters, she may label him homosexual. If he does so "too soon" she may think, "All he wants is my body."

The female may also experience conflict over how much, how soon. For example, if she does not allow the male to engage in sexual behavior soon in the relationship, he may not see her again. If she gives too much too soon, he may label her promiscuous and establish a body-centered rather than person-centered relationship with her.

Another conflict may involve the desire of the female to initiate sexual behavior even though she may feel that it is socially inappropriate to do so. Many females are appalled at the social stigma of being a "bad" girl if they demonstrate an interest in sex. This stigma will change as males begin to accept a wider range of behavior (social and sexual) in the female.

"Sex Is All We've Got"

My partner and I get along great sexually. However, we don't seem to have anything else in common. Although I am happy now with our present relationship, I am fearful that after we are married we will get tired of the sex and there will be nothing else for us to share. What can I do?

Sex is transferable. This implies that you are capable of having a satisfactory sexual relationship with many people. In view of this fact, you might ask yourself, "How many facets (sexual, intellectual, social, recreational) of a relationship do I choose to share with the person I marry?" If you value having a number of interests in common (intellectual, social, academic, and so on), you must develop some of his interests and he some of yours. Otherwise, identify and pursue a partner with whom you already share a wider range of interests. You are wise to avoid a marital relationship that is based only on sex. One middle-aged mother told her engaged daughters, "Everything gets old if you do it often enough—even sex."

Married Person

A married person has asked me to go out with him. What should I do?

Ask yourself if you want to become involved in a relationship that is not mutual. Married people, by definition, are committed to someone else. If it is important to you that the relationship in which you become involved is mutual, select someone who is free to commit himself. One way for you to express your positive feelings for the married person, yet not get involved with him while he is committed to someone else, is to tell him that you are interested in seeing him but that you will only do so when he is legally separated from his spouse. In this way, you are assured that the married person is serious about leaving his mate, which opens the possibility that he may be serious about you.

SUMMARY

Considerable differences have existed in male and female sexual behavior and attitudes. Traditionally, males only had premarital intercourse with females they did not love, while females only had premarital intercourse with males they did love and were committed to marry. Current heterosexual behavior reflects a continued demise in this double standard and a concomitant acceptance of permissiveness-with-affection. The latter normally does not necessitate an understanding of a permanent relationship (marriage) for intercourse to occur.

Although intercourse outside marriage will continue to increase, marriage remains the only culturally approved form of sexual behavior. Homosexual, extramarital, premarital, and "unmarried" sex lack complete social approval. In this sense, marriage legitimizes sexual behavior. Although few people consciously marry for sex, and fewer would verbalize this motivation, it remains a major social and cultural influence on marriage.

Love and sex are not the only motivations for marriage. In Chapter 9, we will discuss pregnancy, rebound, rebellion, and escape (and several other reasons) as alternative motivations for marriage. These are usually considered negative reasons for getting married.

STUDY QUESTIONS

1. Defend the position that actual or promised sexual exchange is a prerequisite to a commitment to marry.

2. How have males traditionally regarded sex and love? Give evidence to support your views.

3. What is homosocial behavior? Give an example to illustrate the concept.

4. Discuss when male masturbation begins, how often it occurs, and why. Comment on the use of fantasy during male masturbation.

5. How is petting defined? Can pregnancy occur if a couple limit their sexual behavior to petting only? Explain.

6. Explain the various premarital sexual standards. What is the most acceptable standard among college students?

7. How has the female traditionally viewed love and sex? How has this changed?

8. Review the findings of Clifford in her study of female masturbation. Mention incidence, frequency, technique, reasons, duration of a mastubatory session, fantasy and frequency of climax.

9. How may petting before marriage affect the sexual response of the woman after marriage?

10. Compare the incidence trends of male and female premarital intercourse.

11. What did Whitehurst report about the reaction of university females to losing their virginity?

12. Discuss the female orgasm in terms of the cognitive and physiological processes. Describe the controversy over the vaginal versus the clitoral orgasm.

13. What answer was given to each of the questions presented in the last section of this chapter? Evaluate each of these answers.

BIBLIOGRAPHY

BELL, R. R. Response to article, *The double standard* by Ronald M. Mazur, *Sexual Behavior*, November, 1972, p. 48.

BELL, R. R. and CHASKES, J. B. Premarital sexual experience among coeds, 1958 and 1968. *Journal of Marriage and the Family*, 1970, **32**, 81–84.

BRODERICK, C. Marriage and Family Counseling Center, University of Southern California, Personal communication, 1972. Published as *Zu Einer Typologie Von Verhaltensmustern Bei Der Brautwerbung In Den USA* in *Soziologie der Familie*. Used by permission of the author.

CANNON, D. L. and LONG, R. Premarital sexual behavior in the sixties. *Journal of Marriage and the Family*, 1971, **33**, 36–49.

CHRISTENSEN, H. T. and GREGG, C. F. Changing sex norms in America and Scandinavia. *Journal of Marriage and the Family*, 1970, **32**, 616–27.

CLAYTON, R. R. Religious orthodoxy and premarital sex. *Social Forces*, 1969, **47**, 469–74.

CLIFFORD, R. Female masturbation in sexual development and clinical application. Doctoral dissertation. Department of Psychology, State University of New York, 1973, in preparation. Used by permission.

DAVIS, M. *The sexual responsibility of women*. New York: Permabooks, 1954, pp. 23–24.

EASTMAN, W. F. First intercourse. *Sexual Behavior*, March, 1972, 23–27.

EHRMANN, W. W. Premarital sexual behavior and sex codes of conduct with acquaintances, friends, and lovers. *Social Forces*, 1959, **38**, 158–64.

GAGNON, J. H. and SIMON, W. *Sexual conduct: The social sources of human sexuality*. Chicago: Aldine Publishing Co., 1973.

HATCH, G. Patterns of affection in dating approved by L.D.S. students. Unpublished Master's Thesis, Brigham Young University, Provo, Utah, 1968.

HERR, S. Research study on behavioral patterns in sex and drug use on the college campus. *Adolescence,* 1970, **5,** 1–16.

HUNT, M. M. *The natural history of love.* New York: Alfred A. Knopf, 1959, p. 319.

JOHNSON, C. E. (ed.). *Sex in human relationships. Columbus,* Ohio: Charles E. Merrill Publishing Company, 1970, p. 51.

KAATS, G. R. and DAVIS, K. E. The dynamics of sexual behavior of college students. *Journal of Marriage and the Family,* 1970, **32,** 390–99.

KATZ, J., and associates. *No time for youth.* New York: Jossey-Bass, 1968.

KINSEY, A. C., POMEROY, W. B., and MARTIN, C. E. *Sexual behavior in the human male.* Philadelphia: W. B. Saunders, 1948.

KINSEY, A. C., POMEROY, W. B., MARTIN, C. E., and GEBHARD, P. H. *Sexual behavior in the human female.* Philadelphia: W. B. Saunders, 1953.

KIRKENDALL, L. A. *Premarital intercourse and interpersonal relations.* New York: Julian Press, 1961.

LIPTON, L. Sexual research on campus. In *Sex and human relationships,* edited by Cecil E. Johnson. Columbus, Ohio: Charles E. Merrill Publishing Company, 1970, p. 51.

LUCKEY, E. B. and NASS, G. D. Comparison of sexual attitudes in an international sample of college students. *Medical Aspects of Human Sexuality,* 1972, **6,** 66–107.

MACE, D. *Getting ready for marriage.* Nashville: Abingdon Press, 1972.

MACKLIN, E. D. Heterosexual cohabitation among unmarried college students. *The Family Coordinator,* 1972, **21,** 463–72.

MORRIS, D. *Intimate behavior.* New York: Random House, Inc., 1971.

MOSHER, D. L. and CROSS, H. F. Sex-guilt and premarital sexual experiences of college students. *Journal of Consulting and Clinical Psychology,* 1971, **36,** 274.

REISS, I. L. Premarital sexuality: Past, present and future. In *Readings on the Family System,* edited by Ira L. Reiss. New York: Holt, Rinehart and Winston, 1972.

———. Toward a sociology of the heterosexual love relationship. *Marriage and Family Living,* 1960, **22,** 139–45.

ROBINSON, I. E., KING, K., and BALSWICK, J. O. The premarital sexual revolution among college females. *The Family Coordinator,* 1972, **21,** 189–94.

SAXTON, L. *The individual, marriage, and the family.* Belmont, California: Wadsworth Publishing Company, 1972.

SCANZONI, J. *Sexual bargaining.* Englewood Cliffs, New Jersey: Prentice-Hall, Inc., 1972.

SCHOFIELD, M. *The sexual behavior of young people.* Boston: Little, Brown and Company, 1965.

SIMON, W. and GAGNON, J. Psychosexual development. In *Human sexuality: Contemporary perspectives,* edited by Eleanor S. Morrison and Vera Borosage. Palo Alto, California: National Press Books, 1973, p. 3.

STEPHENS, W. H. *Reflections on marriage.* New York: Thomas Y. Crowell, 1968.

VREELAND, R. S. Sex at Harvard. *Sexual Behavior,* February, 1972, 2–10.

WHITEHURST, R. H. Losing virginity: Some contemporary trends. *Medical Aspects of Human Sexuality,* 1973, **1,** 335–41. Used by permission.

ZELNICK, M. and KANTER, J. F. Sexuality, contraception, and pregnancy among young unwed females in the United States. Final report to the Commission on Population Growth and the American Future, United States Government Printing Office, Washington, D.C., 1972.

9

Other Reasons for Marriage

*Einstein himself has given various accounts
of why he did, in fact, marry her. One old
friend to whom he confided his own account,
says, "How it came about he doesn't know
himself," and to another he said that he married
despite his parents' determined opposition, out
of a feeling of duty. In old age, he also tried
to rationalize his actions, claiming that what he
called this tragedy in his life probably explained
his immersion in serious work.*

RONALD W. CLARK [1]

Many people look back at their marriage and try to sort out reasons for it.
Like Einstein, they may become confused. Identifying a specific motive for
marriage is difficult. The cultural bias toward marriage often insures that
people marry rather than live together (permanently) or remain single.
However, given that marriage is the most frequent "choice," some motives
for marriage may have negative consequences. This does not imply that
there is any one or best reason for marriage, only that some reasons may
have more positive consequences than others. For example, a marriage for
companionship may have more positive consequences than a marriage
because of a premarital pregnancy. The latter implies that there is no
choice, only a desperate attempt to achieve social acceptability for parenthood through marriage. This reason, and others, are discussed in this
chapter.

[1] Ronald W. Clark, *Einstein: The Life and Times,* Copyright © 1971 by Ronald W. Clark. Used with permission of the publisher, Thomas Y. Crowell Company,
Inc.

PREGNANCY

About one-fourth of all marriages are attended by the fetus (Broderick and Hicks, 1970). It is probable that many of these marriages would never occur had the female not become pregnant. Although an abortion is now a legal alternative, some couples decide to get married or advance the date of the wedding. The Institute for Sex Research estimates that in 20 percent of the premarital pregnancy cases where the female is under 20, marriage will occur (Gebhard, 1958).

Research on these marriages is convincing. Studies consistently show a relationship between a premarital pregnancy and unhappiness in marriage (Christensen and Meissner, 1953; Christensen, 1963; Monahan, 1960; Geismar and La Sorte, 1963; Rountree, 1964). In one study, the authors concluded that marriages forced by premarital pregnancy have double the divorce rate of ordinary marriages (Christensen and Meissner, 1953). Although the premarital pregnancy itself does not result in happiness or unhappiness in marriage, the effects may have negative consequences for several reasons:

(1) The marriage is forced to occur at a time not previously planned. Although the couple may have decided to get married, the time of the marriage may have been radically updated. The clock is turned forward without allowing for the experiences and interaction which would have occurred had the clock been allowed to run its normal cycle.

(2) Babies are expensive. The cost of prenatal care, delivery, and aftercare services will total at least $1,534 the first year (*Population and the American Future,* 1972). If the couple has a steady income, this expense will be no problem. However, some couples must eat bologna and peaches to save money for their utility bills. For them, the expense of a baby is overwhelming.

(3) Babies shatter goals. If the couple had intended to complete their college educations (although they can still do so after the birth of the baby), the probabilities are decreased that their plans may be realized.

(4) The in-law relationship may be marred. In many cases, the in-law relationship begins on a jagged edge when the premarital pregnancy is discovered.

In spite of these possible negative consequences, a premarital pregnancy does not necessarily result in an unhappy relationship. One husband said, "Her pregnancy depressed the hell out of both of us and was a mess with our families. It took us three years to recover, but we made it. We love our little girl and each other."

Faced with a pregnancy though unmarried, there are four alternatives:

1. Get married and keep the baby.
2. Stay single and keep the baby.
3. Give the baby up for adoption.
4. Have an abortion.

In regard to abortion, the Supreme Court, in a 1973 decision, ruled that: (a) During the first three months of pregnancy, abortion is strictly a matter to be decided by a woman and her doctor and must be free of interference by the state; (b) After the third month of pregnancy, a state may regulate abortion procedures, but only in the interest of the pregnant woman's physical safety; and (c) After the fetus becomes viable, about 10 weeks before delivery, a state may prohibit abortion except when a physician decides that it is necessary to preserve the woman's physical or mental health.

If you experience a premarital pregnancy [2] and are unsure what to do, make an appointment with an experienced counselor who will help you decide which option may be best for you. If a counselor is not available to you, you might consider reading a most helpful book by Dr. David Mace, *Abortion: An Agonizing Decision,* Nashville, Tennessee, Abingdon Press, 1972.

REBOUND

After she told me she wouldn't marry me, I became desperate. I called up an old girlfriend to see if I could get the relationship going again. We were married three weeks later. I know it was foolish but I couldn't seem to stop myself.

Marriage on the rebound results when you try to get someone to marry you immediately after another person has terminated a relationship with you. It is a frantic attempt to establish your desirability in the eyes of the partner who just dropped you. In effect, you are sending a message to the other partner, "I am a worthy person. Someone does love me."

To marry on the rebound is questionable because the marriage occurs in reference to the previous partner and not in reference to the partner being married. In reality, you are using the person you intend to marry to establish yourself as the winner in the previous relationship.

To avoid the negative consequences of marrying on the rebound, you should wait until the negative memories of your past relationship have been replaced by positive aspects of your current relationship. In other words,

---

[2] A missed period does not necessarily indicate pregnancy. Consult a physician before assuming that you are pregnant.

marry when the satisfaction of being with your current partner outweighs any feelings of revenge.

REBELLION

A sophomore majoring in physical education, whose parents wanted him to go to medical school, said,

> I am sick of my parents telling me what to do. They don't like Judy because she didn't go to college and because her dad works on the line in a factory. I love her. We will marry and take our chances.

Marriage for rebellion results when your parents say "no" and you say "yes." In a rebellious marriage, you demonstrate your control over your decisions and what you do with your life. As in marriage on the rebound, your marriage is in reference to your parents, not your partner. In a sense, you are using your partner to get back at your parents by showing them that you can win.

It is important to keep in mind that there is no real contest between you and your parents. You will win. Your parents will lose. Marriage in our culture is an individual decision (assuming that the requisite legal requirements have been met) over which parents have little control. You can marry whomever you choose. The issue of control is unrealistic since you are in complete control.

Parents who forbid their son or daughter to date a particular person may actually be encouraging more intense love feelings between the partners. One study demonstrated that parental interference increased the romantic love feelings of the partners for each other (Driscoll, Davis, and Lipetz, 1972).

To avoid marriage for rebellion, separate the issue of control from your assessment of the desirability of marrying your partner at this time. Once you clear away the control issue, you are left with the necessity of carefully evaluating the desirability of marrying your partner. Chapter Two may be useful in helping you to discover the type of person your partner is and whether or not you want to marry him (her). Assessing the desirability of marrying your partner is quite a separate issue from trying to win a power struggle with your parents.

ESCAPE

A partner may marry to escape an unhappy home situation. The parents are often defined as oppressive, overbearing, and unhappy. Their continued bickering may be highly aversive, causing the partner to marry as an escape.

A family with an alcoholic parent is an example of another escape situation. One coed said:

> I couldn't wait to get away from home. Ever since my dad died, my mother has been drinking and watching me like a hawk. "Be home early, don't drink, watch out for those horrible men," she would always say. I admit it. I married the first guy that would have me. Marriage was my ticket away from that bitch.

Marriage for escape can be obviated by continuing the relationship with the partner until mutual love and respect, rather than the desire to escape an unhappy situation, becomes the dominant force propelling you toward marriage. In this way, you can evaluate the marital relationship in terms of its own potential rather than solely as an alternative to an unhappy situation.

PHYSICAL APPEARANCE

When you attempt to get your friend a blind date, one of the first questions you are likely to be asked is, "What does he (she) look like?" The concern for personal appearance permeates our culture. Most advertisements display an obvious bias toward youth and beauty. Observe the age and appearance of people in the next few advertisements you see on television and in magazines.

Not only is a concern for personal appearance demonstrated in the mass media, your peers probably support the idea that youth and beauty are most desirable. For example, your friends may often comment on the attractiveness of your date or partner. Such statements as "He is handsome"; "She's a knockout"; and "What a bombshell" imply a concern for and interest in physical appearance. In effect, your peers specify the most desirable persons to date, and often define them in terms of their physical attractiveness.

The importance that college youth attach to physical attractiveness is unmistakable. Walster, *et al.* (1966) arranged a "blind date" dance for 752 freshmen at the University of Minnesota. During intermission (about two and a half hours into the dance), each of the students completed a confidential questionnaire detailing how he liked his partner and whether he intended to date her again. Walster noted that the only criteria given for deciding to ask the partner for a future date was physical attractiveness. In another study, Silverman (1971) studied twenty couples and asked each partner to rate the physical attractiveness of the other. He concluded that there was an extraordinarily high degree of similarity in physical attractiveness between dating partners and that this was a critical variable in determining who dated whom. Males were more likely to stress the importance of physical attractiveness than females.

As noted in Chapter 8, much dating behavior is homosocial—the partner is dated in reference to the same-sex peers rather than in reference to the partner (Gagnon and Simon, 1973). One male said, "I am going to marry her because she is the most beautiful girl I have ever seen. When we walk into a room together I get the feeling that other males in the room are jealous and envious of me because she is with me. I love to have other males tell me how lucky I am to be with such a beautiful woman." Dating is a social experience in which the two people are available for observation by others; their choice of an attractive partner enables them to achieve status among their peers (Waller, 1938).

Some research on the relationship between dating and marrying beautiful people has been conducted by Berscheid and Walster (1972). They studied girls who were identified as beauties in their college yearbooks 25 years ago. A consistent relationship was found among these college queens and marital *unhappiness*. Many of the husbands reported that they had been cheated. They mused that one of the primary reasons for their marrying the partner was her beauty and that when this began to fade, there was little left.

Marrying *solely* for physical appearance and for the approval of others is likely to have negative consequences. Not only does marrying for beauty imply that other people are greatly concerned about whom you marry (are they really?), it also implies that the beauty of your partner is enough to sustain the relationship over time (is it?). One male who had dated a beautiful girl for a period of two years said, "We argued so much that the way I saw her changed. She wasn't pretty at all."

LONELINESS

A divorced male in his late 30's said, "I don't want to grow old alone." In a society in which over 93 percent of its members marry, he felt sad not to be involved in a stable commitment for life. If you are contemplating marrying someone to escape being lonely the rest of your life, consider two phenomena about loneliness and marriage: (1) Even though you are married, you can still be lonely, and (2) you can be intimately involved with someone and not be married. In regard to marital loneliness, a wife said, "He hasn't touched me since Thanksgiving." She detailed a story of utter loneliness in which her husband was physically present in the home (he ate his meals, slept, watched television, and read the newspaper there) but did not interact with her on an intimate, personal basis. She said, "He's busy with his job and golf." Marriage does not make peple intimate; marriage is only an agreement that two people make at one point in their lives to spend time together. Feelings of intimacy develop as a function of how they spend this time.

A single female in her middle 50's said, "I guess there are worse things in life than being single." The friend, to whom she was talking, replied, "That's right. They call it marriage."

PITY

Some partners marry because they feel guilty about terminating a relationship with someone who is no longer reinforcing. The boyfriend of a coed got drunk one Halloween evening and began to light fireworks on the roof of his fraternity house. As he was running away from a Roman candle he had just ignited, he tripped and fell off the roof. He landed on his head and was in a coma for three weeks. A year after the accident his speech and fine muscle coordination were still adversely affected. The girl said that she did not love him any more but felt guilty about terminating a relationship now that he had become physically afflicted. She was ambivalent. She felt it was her duty to marry her fiancé, but her emotional feelings were no longer love feelings.

In such a situation where one partner loses a limb, becomes brain damaged, or is physically affected so that a normal physical life is impossible, it is important to keep the issue of pity separate from the advisability of contracting the marriage, considering the circumstances. The decision to marry should be based on factors other than pity or gratitude to the partner. This is a value judgment based on the potential long-term negative consequences of contracting a relationship in which one partner has become afflicted late in the courtship process. Although the short-term consequences of marrying one's afflicted fiancé may be positive in that the partner can avoid the guilt of withdrawal and be steadied by the idea that "I did the responsible thing," the long-term consequences may have a debilitating effect on the relationship. If thoughts such as, "I married only half a person" arise, and if living with an afflicted person becomes very difficult to cope with over time, the long-term consequences may be quite negative. It is very important to accurately assess the way you feel about your partner if he or she has experienced a physical impairment.

Should you be the one who becomes afflicted, you must determine if your partner is marrying you out of pity. Your partner may communicate to you that you should be appreciative that he (she) married you because no one else would have you. Of course, the short- and long-term consequences may be positive. A partner may respond to the other's physical impairment as a fact of life and consider the impairment a challenge to an already positive relationship.

Injury may not be the only source of pity. For example, if one partner wants to terminate the relationship (for whatever reason), the other may cry and get the partner to feel sorry for him. This sullen behavior may create feelings of pity in the partner to continue the relationship—a dubious reason for doing so.

SOCIAL PRESSURE

Social pressure for marriage may come from many sources and may be direct or indirect. Parents have traditionally been concerned that their children marry when they reach adulthood. Although your parents may not hassle you about marriage while you are completing your education, as your college years come to a close, they may increase the pressure by communicating in both subtle and more direct ways that "it is time for you to quit fooling around and to get married." In effect, they project that your life will be unhappy unless you are married.

Your roomate and friends may exert a more indirect yet powerful influence. For example, the marriages of your roommate and friends will influence you to think about your future in regard to persons you might marry at this time. The fact that "everyone is getting married" communicates a "rightness" about marriage which increases the pressure on you to be "normal." [3] Without knowing why, you might begin to feel depressed or saddened if you are not soon to be married. This feeling will be a result of the social system in which you are presently immersed. On the other hand, your roommate and friends may not be involved and may have verbalized no intention of marrying in the immediate future. These behaviors will influence you to delay marriage in the same way that your marrying roommate and friends will influence you to marry.

Your siblings may also exert a subtle influence on your decision to marry. As with friends and roommates, the normalcy of marriage is a function of observing others engaging in that behavior. If you have an older brother or sister contemplating marriage or if they are presently married, they may exert subtle pressure on you to "settle down."

The opposite may be just as true. A twenty-eight-year-old single stewardess had an obvious influence on her eighteen-year-old sister's choice of life style. The younger sister verbalized the merits of being a career

---

[3] Traditionally, this feeling has been described as "Senior panic."

woman and had applied for and been accepted by the stewardess school for a major airline. Her sister's example had taught her there are other options in life than marriage, baby, and home-baked cookies.

In effect, all forms of social pressure to marry convey the same theme, "Marriage is what normal people do and you should be normal." Anthropology teaches that what is normal varies from time to time and culture to culture. The normalcy of long hair, short skirts, and blue jeans depend on the person defining the behavior and how many people are engaging in that behavior. In regard to the person defining the behavior, a conservative middle-aged Baptist may view smoking pot quite differently from a nineteen-year-old Unitarian. In regard to the number of people engaging in a specific behavior, if 90 percent of college males wear their hair over their ears, this behavior is considered normal for the college student. In the same way, if only a few males wear butch or burr or short haircuts, this behavior is unusual and "not normal." Hence, the appropriateness of your getting married at a particular time can only be defined in terms of those people who feel that it is appropriate.

POSITIVE "REASONS" FOR MARRIAGE

Just as certain reasons for marrying may have undesirable consequences, marrying for companionship, emotional security, and children may have more positive consequences. Marriage is regarded as one of the most socially approved unions to maintain the feelings of closeness with another human being over time. In this way, the need to belong to someone else is satisfied. A young university English teacher said, "Half the people I dated last year wouldn't walk across the street to say hello to me today. They are involved with someone else. Marriage helps to insure that not only will I be caring about someone next year, but that someone will be caring about me."

Marriage for emotional security is related to marriage for companionship. The former implies that a person seeks the stable structure of marriage to help insure the maintenance of a close interpersonal emotional relationship over time. Married people, by definition, are more committed to each other than people who are living together (see Chapter 5). One married banker said, "I'm glad I'm married. I need it to keep me from doing something foolish." He then explained that there had been times that he had considered leaving his wife but because of the "red tape of getting divorced" he did not. Because of their commitment (personal, legal, social) to stay with each other, this couple managed to resolve their differences and now experience what they regard as a great relationship.

Being secure with a partner is not the same as being chained to that partner. The secure relationship implies a commitment to develop a good relationship. The two partners are facing each other. In a chained relationship, each partner is facing outwards and is desperate to withdraw from the mate. The broken chains are called divorce.

Although most people probably do not consciously marry specifically to have children, they regard children as a valuable part of married life. Although some choose to have children outside of marriage, doing so is considered deviant by our society. Ninety percent of all married couples have children. To be married and have a family is still the American ideal which is sought by the majority of people. Although great variations exist, from living together with children to being married without them, the mainstream of society subscribes to the ideal. The benefits of love, sex, companionship, emotional security, and children can be enjoyed without marriage. But marriage provides the social approval and structure for experiencing these phenomena with the same person over time.

TERMINATING A RELATIONSHIP

After reviewing your positive and negative motivations for marriage, and after evaluating your partner as a potential spouse, you may decide to terminate the relationship. A university cheerleader said, "I have decided that it would be best for my partner and me to break up. I have tried to break up with him before, but we keep getting back together. How can I break the relationship permanently?" Some guidelines for ending a relationship may be helpful:

1. Decide that terminating the relationship is what you want to do. This necessitates careful thought, and implies that the alternative to breaking up is to improve your relationship. (Part Four deals with establishing and maintaining the relationship you desire.) Once you break up with your partner in the suggested manner, it should be difficult to reestablish the relationship.

2. Assuming that you have decided to end your relationship, prepare for the "phone-booth response." After having been formally engaged to a girl for nine months, I decided to terminate the relationship. The day after I had told her that it would be best that we not continue the relationship (translate, I wanted out), I became extremely anxious and upset— almost nauseous. I was miserable. I was like a whimpering dog with distemper. To alleviate my misery, I walked to a phone booth near my apartment, placed a dime in the appropriate slot, and called my ex-girlfriend with the hope of reestablishing the relationship. I received a busy signal. I took this busy signal to be a "message from the gods" that I was to get

out of the phone booth and try to calm myself so as not to call her again.

This phone-booth response is typical of the reaction which occurs after a relationship is terminated. Immediately following the termination of a reinforcer (girlfriend), misery, unhappiness, and a frustrated feeling of loneliness occur. One way to reduce temporarily the unpleasant feeling is to reestablish the relationship with the reinforcer. Although this is a temporary solution for reducing the discomfort, it has a long-term negative consequence. After the exciting make-up period is over, the likelihood of reexperiencing the same unhappy relationship is great. This is because issues which led to the break up of the relationship usually are not resolved during the make-up period.

After I left the phone booth, I went to see a counselor friend who spent several hours encouraging me to think about the long- and short-term consequences of calling my ex-girlfriend again. It was obvious that returning to the relationship would have a very undesirable long-term consequence. In a few days we would be arguing again over the same unresolved issues.

After deciding to terminate the relationship, prepare for the phone-booth response by planning to be with a friend immediately after you break up. In most cases, a close friend will help keep you in balance until the crisis subsides. If a close friend is not available, consult a counselor. Tell him or her you need support through implementing a difficult decision. You will get the help you need.[4]

3. After you are certain that you want to break rather than improve the relationship with your partner and after you have prepared for the phone-booth response, plan a short discussion with your partner at a place from which you can easily withdraw. The apartment or dorm of the person with whom you are breaking up (not your own apartment) is a good place if you have a bike or car with which to get away. Couples who break up at the drive-in theater describe the ride home as unbearable. After you make it clear that you want out of the relationship, go.

4. Explain the reason for breaking the relationship in terms of your own values. For example, a student majoring in business administration told his fiancée that he wanted to marry a career woman. Since she was a home economics major who wanted to get married and rear babies, it was

---

[4] You might contact The American Association of Marriage and Family Counselors (225 Yale Avenue, Claremont, California 91711) or The National Alliance for Family Life (10734 Paramount Boulevard, Suite 20, Downey, California 90241) to identify qualified marriage counselors in your area. Also, the local affiliate of the Family Service Association of America, or your local mental health organization can direct you to a counselor. Other possibilities are the Department of Psychology, the Department of Sociology, or the Counseling Center of your college or university.

hopeless. Rather than tell her that he didn't love her any more, he told her that their values were different. Another example is that of a senior majoring in religion who told her boyfriend that she wanted to marry a practicing Christian, which her pot-smoking, agnostic was not. Explaining the break in terms of your own values allows the partner to save face by feeling that your values are incompatible.

5. Make the break final. If your goal is to terminate the relationship, it is important to do so completely. After explaining your "reasons," tell your partner that you do not want to talk with him or be with him again. Although this may sound cruel, it is more cruel to allow your partner to believe that there is a chance for your relationship to revive. You will keep that hope alive in your partner if you allow for a "let's be friends" type of relationship. Within a week you will be having coffee and donuts at the campus Union, looking into each other eyes, and the relationship (which you decided to break) will resume again.

If you are not "strong enough" to break your relationship in person (because you think your partner can talk you into maintaining the relationship), write a letter explaining your reasons for terminating the relationship and state that you do not want to talk with or be with your partner again. Although you may feel that this is a cowardly way to break the relationship, the issue is to break it. Terminating a relationship is like sky diving, we don't get much practice at it.

6. Seek out another relationship. One of the quickest ways to get over one relationship is to become meaningfully involved in another. "But I could never love anyone as much as I do him" remarked Ingrid, the editor of the university newspaper. Only after she met Robert (a new reporter) did she realize that it was possible to feel very deeply about someone else.

SUMMARY

Some reasons for marriage may have negative consequences. A premarital pregnancy may cause the couple to update the wedding which may prevent them from learning more about each other to assess the desirability of getting married.

Rebounding is as questionable a prelude to marriage as rebelling against or escaping from one's parents. Each of these motives for marriage is in reference to someone other than the person being married.

Physical appearance is a seductively attractive motive for marriage. The cultural emphasis on youth and beauty makes people who are good-looking almost irresistable as marital choices. Sometimes only after marriage is the person evaluated on the basis of qualities other than physical appearance.

Although pregnancy, rebound, rebellion, escape, physical appearance, loneliness, pity, and social pressure may provide a poor basis for marriage in some relationships, others may flower in spite of these questionable motives. For example, regardless of *why* the partners marry, if they exhibit the qualities of flexibility, maturity, and patience in marriage, have some education and money, they are likely to share an enjoyable relationship together.

In regard to your marriage, you might assess your willingness to marry at this time on the basis of predicted long- and short-term consequences. You should marry if you choose, whom you choose, when you choose, and why you choose, This freedom of choice, however, entails a responsibility to separate extraneous issues (pregnancy, rebound, rebellion, escape, personal appearance, loneliness, pity, and social pressure) from the one issue of your belief that both you and your partner will be happier, not only now, but in the future should you choose to contract the relationship.

If you decide that marriage with your partner is unwise, consider the alternatives of improving the relationship before deciding to marry, contracting a potentially unhappy marriage, or terminating the relationship. If you decide to end the relationship, do so with as much preparation as you would have made for the previously desired wedding: be firm in your decision, prepare for the phone-booth response, select a discussion site from which you can easily withdraw, explain the break in terms of your values, and make the break final. The consequence for terminating an unsalvageable relationship is the opportunity to become involved in a new relationship which may have a more hopeful prognosis.

STUDY QUESTIONS

1. How may a marriage which results from a premarital pregnancy experience unusual strain? Describe four potential problem areas.

2. What are the four alternatives if a female becomes premaritally pregnant?

3. What do marriages for reasons of rebound, rebellion, and escape have in common?

4. Why is marrying solely for physical appearance questionable?

5. Discuss the experience of loneliness in marriage and the feeling of involvement (companionship) out of marriage.

6. Discuss the long- and short-term consequences of marrying for reasons of pity.

7. Explain the statement, "All forms of social pressure to marry convey the same theme."
8. Discuss three reasons for marriage which may have positive consequences.
9. Outline and discuss a plan for terminating an unsalvageable relationship.

BIBLIOGRAPHY

BERSCHEID, E. and WALSTER, E. Beauty and the beast. *Psychology Today,* March, 1972, p. 74.

BRODERICK, C. and HICKS, M. Toward a typology of behavior patterns exhibited during courtship in the United States. *Sociology of the Family,* 1970, **14,** 473–85. This article was originally published in German.

CHRISTENSEN, H. T. Child spacing analysis via record linkage: New data plus a summing up from earlier reports. *Marriage and Family Living,* 1963, **25,** 272–80.

CHRISTENSEN, H. T. and MEISSNER, H. H. Studies in child spacing: Premarital pregnancy as a factor in divorce. *American Sociological Review,* 1953, **18,** 641–44.

COOMBS, R. H. and KENKEL, W. F. Sex differences in dating aspirations and satisfaction with computer-selected partners. *Journal of Marriage and the Family,* 1966, **28,** 62–66.

DRISCOLL, R., DAVIS, K., and LIPETZ, M. Parental interference and romantic love: The Romeo and Juliet effect. *Journal of Personality and Social Psychology,* 1972, **24,** 1–10.

GAGNON, J. and SIMON, W. *Sexual conduct: Social sources of human sexuality.* Chicago: Aldine Publishing Co., 1973.

GEBHARD, P. H., *et al. Pregnancy, birth and abortion.* New York: Hoeber-Harper, 1958, p. 65.

GEISMAR, L. L. and LASORTE, M. A. Factors associated with family disorganization. *Marriage and Family Living,* 1963, **25,** 479–81.

MACE, D. *Abortion: An agonizing decision.* Nashville, Tennessee: Abingdon Press, 1972.

MONOHAN, T. P. Premarital pregnancy in the United States: A critical review and some findings. *Eugenics Quarterly,* 1960, **7,** 145.

Population and the American Future, Report of the Commission on Population Growth and the American Future, Washington: U.S. Government Printing Office, 1972, p. 81.

ROUNTREE, G. Some aspects of marriage breakdown in Britain during the last thirty years. *Population Studies,* 1964, **18,** 147–63.

RUSSELL, B. *Marriage and morals*. New York: Horace Liveright, 1929.

SILVERMAN, I. Physical attractiveness and courtship. *Sexual Behavior*, 1971, **1**, 22–25.

WALLER, W. *The family*. New York: Holt, Rinehart and Winston, 1938.

WALSTER, E., ARONSON, V., ABRAHAM, D., and ROTTMAN, L. Importance of physical attractiveness in dating behavior. *Journal of Personality and Social Psychology*, 1966, **5**, 58.

IV

THE HUMAN RELATIONSHIP

Now it is a proper work of a man
to be benevolent to his own kind . . .
MARCUS AURELIUS, Meditations, Book VIII

Enjoyable relationships do not occur by chance. Rather, they occur under certain conditions and not under others. In Chapter 10 we discuss specific problem-solving procedures to reduce role conflict. In the final chapter, the focus is on verbal and non-verbal interpersonal communication in reference to peer and parent relationships. These interpersonal and communication skills are essential in developing and maintaining relationships in or out of marriage.

10

Interpersonal Skills

*People teach each other how to behave and from
these behaviors spring happiness or unhappiness.*

CHARLES H. MADSEN, JR.[1]

Whether you and your partner decide to get married, live together, or stay single, it is helpful to have interpersonal skills to experience enjoyable relationships. The necessity for these skills implies that the behavior and expectations of you and your partner will differ and require adjustment to reduce the strain. For example, if Sally expects John to spend his Sunday afternoons with her while he prefers playing bridge with his male peers, his behavior and her expectations are at odds. Sally feels neglected and John, guilty and nagged. Their happiness is dependent on their skills to resolve or reduce this conflict.

At least five skills are necessary to resolve conflict and continue a positive relationship. These are: listen empathically, identify the problem behavior, understand the behavior, select a plan to resolve the problem, and implement the plan. A specific example is used to illustrate these skills. The

[1] C. H. Madsen, Jr., Department of Psychology, Florida State University. Personal communication, 1973.

151

relationship problem is taken from Cutler and Dyer's (1965) study of 60 couples married less than three years. The primary complaint among the wives was that their husbands were spending too much time away from home.

LISTEN EMPATHICALLY

Empathy involves the ability to experience something from another person's point of view. Empathic listening requires two behaviors: (1) listening to your partner and asking questions so that you develop a complete understanding of how he perceives and feels about the issue you are discussing; and (2) explaining your partner's position to him to assure him and yourself that you understand his position. For example, it is important that Sally ask John to explain his feelings about enjoying an afternoon with his peers. She should then explain, without criticizing, his position to him. This will assure John that she understands the issue from his point of view. It is also important that John ask Sally to explain her feelings about his playing bridge with his friends on Sunday afternoon. He should then tell her how she feels to assure Sally that he understands her feelings.

Be cautious in sharing your feelings. Cutler and Dyer (1965) observed that 50 percent of their couples ended up arguing after an open sharing of ideas. It is crucial that you avoid attacking your partner for his position. Empathic listening involves your gaining a full understanding of your partner's point of view. If either you or your partner becomes upset or defensive, terminate your conversation until another time when tempers have cooled.

IDENTIFY THE PROBLEM BEHAVIOR

Your attitudes and feelings toward your partner are based on his behavior. If your partner criticizes you, lies to you, and is frequently late to meet you, your feelings toward him will be negative. If he compliments you, is honest with you, and is always on time, your feelings for him are more likely to be positive. These examples illustrate that negative feelings in a relationship occur under two conditions: (1) When your partner does something that you do not like (lies to you), and (2) When your partner fails to do something that you like (tell you, "I love you").

When you experience dissatisfaction in your relationship, identify behavior that is or is not occurring which causes you to get angry. Find behavioral causes for your feelings. For example, a wife who said, "He makes me angry," identified four behaviors in which her husband was engaging that upset her: He gambled, drank two six packs every night, criticized her, and provided no foreplay before intercourse. These behaviors were the problem. In the example of Sally and John, John's behavior, spending time away from Sally on Sunday afternoon from noon to 6 p.m., is the problem. When dissatisfaction occurs, identify the behavior in which your partner is engaging that creates those feelings. Until you identify a behavior for your feelings, a solution is almost impossible.

The behavior must be measurable. A "mean person" and "bad attitude" are meaningless accusations unless they can be expressed in specific behavioral terms. For example, an angry male said his fiancée was inconsiderate. When asked for a specific example of her inconsiderateness he said, "When we are watching television together at night, she will go into the kitchen around 10 and fix herself a peanut butter and jelly sandwich and a glass of milk. She then comes back to the den, sits down on the couch, eats the sandwich, drinks her milk, and doesn't ask me if I want something to eat." Being inconsiderate is a vague concept. Failure to ask her partner if he would like an evening snack is a behavior that can be observed and measured. To effectively identify a problem, select a behavior that you can count. This implies that you must be able to see or hear the behavior which is upsetting.

UNDERSTANDING THE BEHAVIOR [2]

After you have identified the behavior your partner is engaging in which upsets you, consider how the behavior was learned and what makes the behavior continue. Interpersonal behavior is learned. The behaviors you exhibit when answering the phone, dining, or talking have been learned. The behaviors your partner exhibits which please or upset you have been learned. In our example, John has learned to spend Sunday afternoon playing bridge with his male friends. It may be helpful for Sally to understand why he engages in this behavior rather than to accuse him of not loving her.

In this section, four basic rules of learning are presented: reward, extinction, punishment, and negative reinforcement. These principles may be used to explain how existing behavior has been learned and how new, more desirable behavior may be developed. The Sunday afternoon conflict between Sally and John is used to illustrate these principles.

[2] This section is based on a discussion by Dr. Jack Turner, Research Director of The Huntsville–Madison County Mental Health Center, Huntsville, Alabama, on marriage management (1973). Used by permission.

Reward

The reward rule says that any behavior which is followed by something pleasant will tend to recur. If you go to your mailbox and find a letter from your boyfriend, letter-seeking behavior has been rewarded. There is an increased probability that you will go to the mailbox again to look for a letter from him. Turning on your radio has been reinforced by listening to enjoyable music in the past. In regard to John's behavior, he derives satisfaction from spending his Sunday afternoons playing bridge with his male friends. From a learning perspective, Sally may view John as wanting to play bridge Sunday afternoon because, in the past, doing so has resulted in a rewarding experience.

A reward is always defined in terms of its effect on behavior. By definition, anything which strengthens the chance that a behavior will recur is a reward. If Sally scolds John for spending Sunday afternoon playing bridge and he begins to play bridge Saturday afternoons too, Sally's scolding has actually reinforced John's spending time away from her. This is true because her scolding resulted in his playing bridge more often.

Sally's scolding John because she thought he would play less bridge illustrates an important concept in learning—projection. In this context, projection means the tendency to assume that other people feel the same as you about what is pleasant (rewarding) and unpleasant (punishing). Since verbal criticism is severely aversive and punishing to Sally, she assumed that it would be so for John. She projected her feelings onto him. However, verbal abuse by Sally is not punishing to John. He enjoys seeing her get upset. He regards it as her caring about him. The point to keep in mind is: what is punishing to one person may be rewarding to another. Only an examination of the *effect* on behavior can determine what is rewarding or punishing.

Another example may be helpful. A coed complained that her boyfriend was always late. She said that each time he was late, she became upset and yelled at him for his tardiness. She assumed (projected) that yelling would stop the negative behavior. However, her boyfriend seemed to be late more often after she began to yell at him. It is clear that her negative comments about his late behavior were actually rewarding, since anything which increases the frequency of a behavior is a reward.

Observe the various behaviors that you like and do not like in your partner. Try to identify the rewards responsible for developing the behaviors and for currently maintaining them. Avoid projecting your own ideas about what "should be rewarding" and look at the effect on behavior.

Extinction

The extinction rule states that when a reward is consistently withdrawn, the behavior stops. This rule is helpful to explain behavior which did occur but has subsequently stopped. For example, Charlie and Maureen had a summer romance at the beach. In the fall, Charlie went to a state university 400 miles away. The first month of their separation, he wrote Maureen frequent letters. During September, she anxiously checked her mailbox for Charlie's letters. Since Charlie became involved in a new relationship, he stopped writing. Maureen continued to go to the mailbox for several days even though Charlie had written her a "Dear-John letter." After two weeks of going to the post office to look at an empty box, Maureen stopped. Her behavior had been extinguished.

Notice that extinction is the opposite of reward. Reward involves giving or presenting something (the letters came); extinction involves withdrawing or taking something away (the letters stopped). Reward increases the chance that a behavior will occur in the future (going to the post office) while extinction decreases the chance that a behavior will occur (stop going to the post office).

The extinction rule may also help you to understand the interaction between Sally and John regarding his playing bridge on Sunday afternoons. Sally no longer asks John to spend Sunday afternoon with her. This implies that John has effectively extinguished her asking by not doing what she asked.

Identify the behaviors you have extinguished in your partner. For example, if you have decided that you do not want to live together, your continued refusal to do so will stop your partner from raising the issue. You might also identify the behaviors your partner has extinguished in you. For example, you may never ask your partner if he would like to go shopping with you since, in the past, he has not reinforced your suggestion.

Punishment

Punishment occurs when something negative happens after a behavior. Something has been punishing if it lowers the chance that the behavior will recur. For example, if John tells Sally that he will leave her should she mention his Sunday afternoon bridge playing again, his threat may be enough to stop Sally's mentioning it.

Like reward, punishment is defined in terms of its actual effect on behavior, not in terms of its assumed, projected effect. If Sally has a decreased probability of mentioning John's playing bridge after he has threatened to leave her, his threat was a punishment. However, if Sally continued to mention his Sunday afternoons, his threat would be a reward (although he may have assumed—projected—that his threat would act as punishment), since her nagging continued.

Negative consequence is another expression for punishment. Later in this chapter, we will discuss how attaching a negative consequence to a behavior can be used to help terminate an undesirable behavior.

Negative Reinforcement

A negative reinforcer is any event which stops something unpleasant. Stepping out of the July sun into an air-conditioned office is negatively reinforcing because it stops the feeling of being hot. Picking up the telephone is negatively reinforcing because it stops the aversive ringing. Beginning in 1972, car manufacturers began to use the principle of negative reinforcement to encourage you to wear your seat belt. If your seat belt is not fastened and you place the gear shift in drive, a loud buzzing will begin. This buzzing will stop when you fasten your seat belt.

The principle of negative reinforcement is not applicable to the case of John and Sally. However, nagging can be explained by this principle. A wife may nag her husband to clean out the car. Each week he does not do so, she increases the frequency and intensity of her request. Finally, her critical remarks become so loud that her husband cleans out the car. His doing so can be understood through the principle of negative reinforcement. His behavior stopped the aversive nagging. The wife's nagging can be explained by the reward rule—her husband did what she asked him to do only after she repeatedly made loud requests (nagged).

How Behavior Is Learned—A Summary

To summarize, reward is the presentation of something pleasant to increase the probability that a behavior will occur. Punishment is the presentation of something unpleasant which decreases the probability that something will occur. Both rewards and punishments are always defined in terms of their effect on behavior. Extinction is withdrawing something positive, while negative reinforcement is withdrawing something negative. Extinction stops behavior and negative reinforcement increases it.

Another interpersonal example illustrating these four principles may be helpful. A chauvinist husband complained that his wife never kept a clean living room. A clean living room was defined as one in which the newspapers were off the floor, the ash trays were emptied, no more than two magazines were on the coffee table, and the *TV Guide* was near the armchair. The husband complained that she had kept a disheveled living room since their marriage. The wife said that her husband had always nagged her about it.

The reward rule suggests that the husband's nagging is the reinforcer for the unkempt living room. Since nagging has increased rather than decreased his wife's house cleaning behavior, it (nagging) is a reward by definition. Even though the husband may have intended his remarks to make her feel bad about not keeping the living room clean, his nagging had the opposite effect. She may enjoy this attention from her husband.

The extinction rule helps to explain why the husband no longer asks his wife in a pleasant way to straighten the living room. He does not do so because she does not reinforce this behavior by doing what he asks. She has extinguished pleasant, asking behavior. The punishment rule does not seem applicable. His nagging is reinforcing (rather than punishing) to her since it increases her non-housecleaning activity.

Negative reinforcement may help to explain the wife's behavior. On occasion, we might guess, the wife does clean the living room. This is in response to her husband's excessive nagging. Hence, when the nagging becomes so extremely aversive, she cleans the living room to stop the nagging. There is nothing mystical about human behavior. This husband has learned to nag, and his wife has learned not to clean the living room.

To review, where a problem exists in your relationship, listen empathically—get inside your partner's head and see the difficulty from his perspective. Next, identify the problem in terms of specific behavior in which either you or your partner is or is not engaging and attempt to explain the problem using the four basic principles of learning. This latter exercise has two functions: (1) it encourages you to explore the ways in which your behavior influences your partner's behavior; and (2) it avoids the judgment that your partner is engaging in undesirable behavior just to be mean and replaces it with the judgment that the behavior is learned.

SELECT A PLAN TO RESOLVE THE PROBLEM

An interpersonal problem may be resolved in one of four ways (Cutler and Dyer, 1965): (1) One partner can change his behavior to meet the expectations of the other. For example, John can spend Sunday afternoons with Sally doing something they both enjoy. (2) One partner can change his expectations of the other. Sally may decide that it is no longer important that John spend his Sunday afternoons with her. She then removes all of her previous expectations of him and does not attempt to induce guilt in him for spending Sunday afternoon with his peers. (3) A mutual adjustment of behavior and expectation can occur. Sally and John may agree that every other week they would spend Sunday afternoon together and, on alternate weeks, John would play bridge with his friends. (4) The partners agree to disagree. This last solution implies that John and Sally stop talking about the issue. John continues to play cards on Sunday and feel somewhat guilty. Sally continues to feel that John should be with her but she does not say anything about it. Each resolved to his own position, they stop discussing it.

With rare exception, a closer relationship results when both partners agree to make some change in behavior or expectation for the relationship. In this way, each partner feels as though he can influence the other. This encourages a willingness to be influenced by the other. To the degree that the partners can influence a change in each other's behavior or expectations, role conflict will be minimized.

IMPLEMENT THE PLAN

You recall from the section "Identify the Problem Behavior" that it is necessary to find a behavioral cause for feelings of irritation, frustration, and anger. It is equally important to identify positive behavioral goals. Rather than tell your partner what you dislike, tell him what you would like him to do in the future. For example, "Stop being late," should be expressed as "Please be on time," and "Stop spending Sunday afternoons away from me," should be expressed as "Please spend some time on Sunday afternoons with me." These positive behavioral goals emphasize the importance of expressing the behavior you would like your partner to exhibit in the future.

Before a couple decide to change a behavior in one partner, they should identify a behavior for the other to change. For example, John said that he would like Sally to compliment him on his bridge playing on Sunday afternoons rather than nag him for playing. Sally's willingness to change one of her behaviors will make John more willing to engage in a behavior to please her. Lederer and Jackson (1968) have discussed the *quid pro quo* of marriage. Their "something for something" implies that each partner should not be expected to do something for nothing. Rather, each is expected to engage in a reciprocal positive behavior for the other.

Hence, in resolving an interpersonal problem, identify two positive behavioral goals to accomplish. Although these goals need not be related to each other (the behavioral goals of John and Sally are related), each partner should agree to change a behavior to make his partner happier in exchange for a behavior the partner will engage in to make him happier. In this way, each can avoid being labeled as the "sick partner" and can feel as though his willingness to change his own behavior or expectations will be met with appreciation as defined by the partner's willingness to change his behavior or expectations.

After each partner agrees to change a behavior, it is important that he also agree to take certain negative consequences for not fulfilling his part of the agreement. It is also helpful to write out the agreement in contract form. This confirms your willingness to improve your relationship. Talking is frequently not as effective as developing a contract to specify how behavior will change in the future.

For example, John agreed that he would spend alternate Sunday afternoons with Sally in exchange for her positive statements to him ("I am glad you enjoy playing bridge") about his bridge game. Should he fail to spend every other Sunday afternoon with her, his punishment would be no cigarettes for two days (he smokes a pack a day). Should Sally fail to make at least one positive statement, it would result in her sitting alone in the closet for one hour (she hated isolation). The agreement contracts were as follows:

John's Agreement

I agree to engage in the following behavior to make our relationship better: *spend every other Sunday afternoon with Sally.* If I fail to engage in this behavior, I agree to the following negative consequence: *no cigarettes for two days.* The purpose of this negative consequence is to encourage me to fulfill my part of the agreement.

Partner _____

Date _____

Sally's Agreement

I agree to engage in the following behavior to make our relationship better: *make one positive statement to John when he returns from card playing on Sunday afternoon.* If I fail to engage in the above behavior, I agree to the following negative consequence: *sit alone in the closet for one hour.* The purpose of this negative consequence is to encourage me to fulfill my part of the agreement.

Partner _____

Date _____

FIGURE 10-1   *John's and Sally's agreements to change their behavior to improve their relationship.*

Other examples of a plan to change behavior may be helpful. A coed agreed that she would be on time to meet her partner for lunch or she would lose the right to talk on the phone and read her mail for 24 hours. A senior nursing student, living with her boyfriend, wanted him to be responsible for keeping their bathroom clean. He agreed to do so and take the negative consequence of using the Gulf service station bathroom if he failed to do so.

Some behaviors occur without a negative consequence attached to them. Some partners find it easy to change a behavior just by deciding to do so. Others experience difficulty beginning a new behavior. To insure success, they assign a negative consequence for failure to perform the agreed behavior. The objective is to get the behavior to occur.

ACME

The Association of Couples for Marriage Enrichment, founded by a couple who have been married over 40 years (David and Vera Mace) is a national and international organization of married couples who unite with other married couples. The objectives of the Association are:

1. To seek together to become equal partners in a loving, sharing, and mutually creative relationship.
2. To join with other ACME members in activities and experiences designed to promote mutual growth and enrichment.
3. To help to provide and to promote in our community effective services to foster better marriages.
4. To work to improve the public image of marriage as a relationship capable of promoting both personal growth and mutual fulfillment (Mace and Mace, 1974).

Married couples concerned about keeping their interpersonal skills at the very highest level might consider uniting with other couples who have the same goals.[3]

SUMMARY

We have discussed a way in which interpersonal role conflict may be resolved. A prerequisite to resolving a disagreement is empathic listening. To the degree that your partner feels that you understand (intellectually and emotionally) his viewpoint, the probability of resolving the conflict increases.

While listening empathically to each other, try to pinpoint specific behaviors that are causing your respective negative feelings. Unless you identify specific behaviors to be changed, there is little hope of resolving your differences.

Once problem behaviors of both partners are identified, analyze the ways in which the behaviors have been learned. How are the four rules of learning (reward, extinction, punishment, and negative reinforcement) operative in the development and continuation of the undesirable behaviors?

Selecting a plan to resolve the problem is the essence of keeping your relationship happy. A complete change in expectation or behavior by either partner, a compromise, or an agreement to disagree (but not to discuss again) are the alternatives for problem resolution. Where the decision is made to change behavior, a negative consequence (for failure to fulfill the agreement) must be established to insure that the desirable behavior occurs. Consequences change behavior when talking does not. Relationship problems which you experience with your partner should be resolved now. Couples who do not resolve their problems, keep them.

[3] Information and membership forms may be obtained by writing to ACME, 403 S. Hawthorne Road, Winston-Salem, N. C. 27103.

STUDY QUESTIONS

1. How will you know if your partner has empathy?

2. Where do the attitudes and feelings you have about your partner come from?

3. Why is it important that the behavior you define as the source of the problem be a behavior that you can measure?

4. Define the four rules of learning. Give an example of each one.

5. Distinguish between negative reinforcement and reward.

6. What are four ways to resolve an interpersonal disagreement?

7. Why is it important to take a negative consequence for failure to engage in the appropriate behavior?

8. Give an example of a problem you have had with your partner and how you could use each of the steps suggested to resolve the problem.

BIBLIOGRAPHY

CUTLER, B. R. and DYER, W. C. Initial adjustment processes in young couples. *Social Forces,* 1965, 195–201.

KNOX, D. *Marriage Happiness: A Behavioral Approach to Counseling.* Champaign, Illinois: Research Press Company, 1971.

KNOX, D. Behavior contracts in marriage counseling. *Journal of Family Counseling,* 1973, **1,** 22–27.

KNOX, D. *Dr. Knox's Marital Exercise Book.* New York: David McKay Company, Inc., forthcoming.

LEDERER, W. J. and JACKSON, D. D. *Mirages of Marriage.* New York: W. W. Norton and Company, 1968.

MACE, D. and MACE, V. *We can have better marriages if we really want them.* Nashville: Abingdon Press, 1974.

MADSEN, C. H., JR. and MADSEN, C. K. *Teaching/Discipline.* Boston: Allyn and Bacon, 1970.

PATTERSON, G. R. *Families.* Champaign, Illinois: Research Press Company, 1971.

RAPPAPORT, A. F. and HARRELL, J. A. A behavioral-exchange model for marital counseling. *The Family Coordinator,* 1972, **21,** 203–11.

STUART, R. B. Operant-interpersonal treatment for marital discord. *Journal of Consulting and Clinical Psychology,* 1969, **33,** 675–82.

TURNER, A. J. Couple and group treatment of marital discord. Paper, presented at Sixth Annual Association for the Advancement of Behavior Therapy, New York, October, 1972.

WATSON, D. L. and THARP, R. G. *Self-Directed Behavior: Self-modification for Personal Adjustment.* Monterey, California: Brooks/Cole Publishing Company, 1972.

11

Communication

The development and continuation of a happy interpersonal relationship requires effective communication. In this chapter, you are encouraged to check the communication wires between you and your partner. Frayed, loose wires can be replaced to insure a clear channel of communication. A well-wired message system will enhance your interpersonal enjoyment.

Communication means more than talking. Communication may be defined as a message one person sends and another receives (Satir, 1967). For example, the message "I love you" may be communicated in a phrase ("I love you"), gesture (outstretched arms), facial expression (pleasant smile), tone of voice (whisper), speed of speech (slow), eyes (attentive), and touch (gentle). Although you use words to transmit the major thrust of your message, the person receiving your message may rely more on other cues. When your partner tells you that he loves you, you may look closely into his eyes for a loving look to confirm those words.

What you say and what you do should always relay the same meaning to avoid confusing the person receiving the message. For example, a coed bewildered her boyfriend by writing him the following note: "Dear Nash: I love you very much and have enjoyed our three years together, but I don't think I should see you again. However, I will be home Friday night if you wish to call. As ever, Marilyn." Nash is rightly confused. In the same letter he is told that: (1) he is loved, (2) Marilyn does not think she should see him again, and (3) she will be waiting for him Friday night. This confusion could be avoided by Marilyn's deciding whether or not she wishes to continue the relationship with Nash and, if so, under what conditions. If she decides to terminate the relationship forever, she should write the following note: "Dear Nash: I want to end our relationship because your continued use of hard drugs makes life unbearable for me. Do not call or see me again." Having written this letter, Marilyn should not answer the phone or agree to see Nash again. Her verbal and behavioral message are the same.

The incongruence of verbal and non-verbal messages also occurs in interpersonal interaction. For example, Dianna may feel jealous when Skip talks about "his old girlfriend." Inadvertently, she may express her disapproval by sulking and withholding physical affection. When Skip asks, "What's wrong?" she replies, "Nothing," although her non-verbal behavior reveals her anger.

EFFECTIVE COMMUNICATION

Each day you transmit several messages to your partner. These verbal messages are either declarative statements, questions, or answers. For effective communication, it is important that your statements are clear and that your questions are honest and direct. It is also important that you answer questions in an honest and direct manner.

Clear Communication

How much does your partner want to listen to a band, see a movie, or eat chicken tonight? One way to clearly assess his desires and communicate your own is to use a ten-point scale. Zero implies no interest in engaging in the activity, whereas ten reflects extreme enthusiasm. For example, one coed recently asked her fiancé, for whom she was preparing dinner, "What is your number for baked chicken?" He replied, "Three." She asked, "How about broiled flounder?" "Ten." He then asked, "What do you think about seeing the campus movie after dinner?" She replied, "Six." He asked, "The new film downtown?" "Nine." They enjoyed flounder and the downtown film. Their communication was clear about how much each wanted to do what.

What happens when the numbers differ? For example, when Jack wants flounder at "ten" and Sylvia wants steak at the same level, is it flounder or steak? Some couples flip a coin. Others alternate: tonight is steak, but Jack wins next time when he and Sylvia conflict at the same level. Still others select a mutually desired alternative—ham.

Of course, on most occasions, the selection of a number between 1 and 10 to express degree of desire is unnecessary. You know how your partner feels about many issues. When an uncertain situation arises, however, consider asking him to rate his desires on a ten-point scale. His numerical answer to your question, "How much?" may be more helpful to you than his answer, "It doesn't matter too much."

Honest and Dishonest Questions [1]

Questions you ask your partner should be honest. An honest question is one in which you do not get angry if your partner gives you an answer different from the one you expect. It is an honest question in the sense that you sincerely want to know the answer and are not offended by a negative response. For example, suppose you ask your partner, "Do you have time to pick up some books at the library for me?" You are asking an honest question if he can say "no" without your getting angry (you really can wait until tomorrow, if he is busy). Another example. Suppose you ask your partner to see a movie tonight. You will be asking an honest question if he can say, "I am sorry, I need to study," without your getting angry. A third example. Suppose you have decided to take your fiancée out to dinner tonight. You ask her, "Where would you like to eat?" If your question is honest she can reply, "The Lobster Inn," which you know will cost ten dollars per person.

A dishonest question is one in which you do get angry at your partner if he gives you an answer contrary to what you expect. If you become angry when your partner responds to the above questions, "No, I don't have time to get your books," "I don't want to see a movie tonight," "I want to go to the Lobster Inn," you have asked dishonest questions. To insure that you are always asking an honest question, ask yourself before you ask the question, "Will I be angry if my partner does not respond as I want?" If your answer is "yes," you will be asking a dishonest question. If your answer is "no," you will be asking an honest question.

To avoid asking a dishonest question, make a declarative statement.

[1] Honest, dishonest, direct, and indirect questions were developed by Dr. Clifford K. Madsen, Department of Music and Dr. Charles H. Madsen, Jr., Department of Psychology, Florida State University, and are used with their permission.

For example, "Let's see the campus film" communicates two messages: (1) you would like to see the film; and (2) you would like your partner to go with you. To insure that your declarative statement does not anger your partner, you might ask him to express his desire to see the movie on the ten-point scale and resolve any differences of desires as discussed under clear communication.

To avoid answering a dishonest question, ask your partner (before answering), "Are you asking an honest question?" If the answer is "no" (a dishonest question has been asked), no answer is necessary since the partner has already decided that he will accept only one answer.

Honest Answers

Questions should not only be asked honestly, they should also be answered honestly. For example, if your partner asks you, "What would you like to do this evening?" and you reply, "Anything," this implies that driving to the local garbage dump and counting Campbell's soup cans would be fine. Another example. If your fiancé wants to know what you would like for supper, and you reply, "Anything will do," your partner may then serve cornflakes and peaches. You may be delighted; you may not. When you have preferences, express them.

Direct Questions

Not only should communication be clear and honest, it should be direct. Ask your partner specifically what you want to know. For example, if you ask, "How do you like my hair?" this implies that you are asking for his opinion about your hair and not about his feelings for you. Hence, if he were to say, "I don't like it," you should not assume that he does not love you since you asked the question about your hair and not about his love for you. If you want to know whether or not he loves you, ask the direct question, "Do you love me?" If you want to know what your partner thinks about your hair, your interest in music, your mother, or your study habits, ask the question. However, do not hold your partner responsible for answering a question that you have not asked.

To insure that your partner is asking a direct question (as opposed to an indirect question), you might ask, "Is that really what you want to know?" In this way, you will know what you are answering, and your partner will be clear about what he is asking. Effective communication is making sure that the message that you send is the same as the message that someone else receives. This necessarily implies clear, honest, and direct communication of messages.

JEALOUSY

Some relationships terminate because of jealousy while other partners develop a clear understanding of the jealousy issue and do not allow it to drive a wedge between them. Jealousy may be defined as a suspicious feeling of a rival's influence. Feelings of jealousy are often expressed in such phrases as, "You really enjoyed dancing with him, didn't you?" and "You don't have to study with her." In effect, the partner is accused of giving too much time and attention to someone else.

Your partner may reward you for the expression of jealous feelings. For example, his typical response to your accusation that he seems to enjoy studying with the girl in his history class will be denial and reaffirmation of love for you. Not only will he tell you that he has no serious intention of becoming involved with her, he will also say that he loves you a great deal. In effect, your partner is keeping your jealous feelings alive by telling you that he loves you. Notice the way your communication is linked together: Accusation followed by reaffirmation of love. He might never tell you of his love for you if you did not make jealous accusations. If you stopped accusing him of other interests, he might stop professing love for you.

If you feel jealous, what evidence do you have for his involvement with someone else? Be aware that his interest in others will occur whether married or single and does not necessarily imply negative feelings for you. If your partner demonstrates this casual interest in someone else, consider the consequences of accusing him of a sexual and emotional investment in that person. An accusation may result in the Pygmalion effect (see Chapter 1.) and encourage him to become more involved with that person or someone else and make your expectation come true.

We have been talking about the partner who feels jealous and have suggested that positive consequences may result from avoiding any accusation. On the other side of the accusation, some partners are continually hounded with expressions of jealousy and are concerned about stopping it.

To effectively terminate the expression of your partner's jealousy you must stop the reinforcement following the jealous statements and assist him in developing more desirable expectations of your behavior. Specifically, if you want to stop your partner from engaging in jealous behavior, consider engaging in the following behaviors: (1) Profess your love verbally and behaviorally when your partner is *not* acting jealous. Make absolutely certain that you have told your partner that you love him and that your behavior demonstrates your words. (At the same time, you should be careful not to give your partner a reason to be jealous. (2) Tell your partner that since you are very much in love with him and have no intention of becoming intimately involved with someone else, you will not talk with him if he expresses a feeling of jealousy. When your partner accuses you of valuing someone else over him, you should terminate the conversation with your partner immediately. For example, if your boyfriend were to accuse you of interest in another male, you should ask him to take you home. You should make it absolutely clear that you do not intend to defend your behavior since you have already stated your intentions in continuing the relationship with your partner.

However, if you do become involved with someone else or think that you would like to, you might simply tell your partner that you are becoming involved with someone else and want to terminate the relationship.

CONFESSING THE PAST

Most relationships have unwritten rules in regard to confessions. Landis and Landis (1973) studied 122 engagements and concluded that although both men and women tend to reveal much about their previous experiences to their fiancés, men tend to reveal more information than do women. For example, whereas 91 percent of the males who had experienced premarital sexual relations told their partners, only 86 percent of the females did so. Another example: 82 percent of the men who had petting experiences with others told their fiancées, whereas only 64 percent of the females did so.

Revealing your past should be based on a careful consideration of the consequences. Will your relationship be happier once this information is known? Will it make any difference? In the Landis (1973) study, 95 percent of both partners felt that revealing their pasts had positive consequences for their relationship.

If you feel the urge to confess a previous experience, consider the alternative of sharing your experience with a professional counselor. This will allow you to drain off feelings of guilt without risking your relationship. The counselor might also assist you in developing a new perspective of your past experience so that the need to confess will be reduced or eliminated.

Some past events should be told. In general, if something in your past has the potential to affect your future relationship, hiding such information may have more negative consequences than revealing it. Venereal disease, a previous marriage, imprisonment, suspected bad heredity, and a child out of wedlock should be told to your partner.[2] Doing so will remove the skeleton rattling in your closet and allow you to interact with your partner without feeling that you have tricked him.

[2] A hidden physical impairment that affects interpersonal functioning should also be revealed. For example, a coed was deaf in one ear. Unless her partner knew of this, he might assume he was getting the "silent treatment."

COMMUNICATION WITH PARENTS

Some students complain that their parents do not understand them and ask, "How can I get my parents to understand how I feel about things?" You may not be able to do so. This is neither a result of your inadequate explanations nor your parents' unwillingness to listen. The confused communication is often a function of the fact that both you and your parents have been exposed to different learning experiences which do not overlap. You are exposed to information and experiences through your classes, movies, music, and interpersonal relationships which may be quite different from those experienced by your parents twenty years ago. It is difficult for most parents to think in terms other than those which approximate their own experiences. For example, you cannot understand what it is like to live in India unless you have lived in India. In the same way, your middle-class, middle-aged parents may not be able to understand what it is like to be a college student at the present time.

This breakdown in communication between the generations is often increased when parents try to interfere in the dating relationships of their children. Some parents express subtle disapproval of their son's or daughter's dating partner, while others try to prohibit all interaction.

Your parents may try to discourage you from dating someone they do not like for three reasons. First, your parents may have been hurt and disappointed in their own dating relationships and do not want these disappointments to happen to you. If your mother was jilted, she may encourage you not to become involved with men. If you father feels that he married too soon (in high school), he may encourage you to delay marriage until your late twenties.

Second, your parents may have friends who have become trapped in unsuccessful relationships. After observing these poor marriages, your parents fear that you may make some of the same mistakes. For example, your parents may have observed a girl who dropped out of school to support her husband end up in an unhappy marriage. It is horrifying for them to think that your behavior may have the same result.

Third, your parents may analyze their own marriage and feel that it is not as happy as they had expected. For example, it is possible that your mother may still feel guilty for having had intercourse before marriage and would like to prevent you from making the "same mistake" (Wake, 1969). Or, your mother may wish that she had finished school rather than marrying at an early age. Since the consequences for her dropping out of school and marrying were negative, she would like you to avoid a similar situation.

To cope with your parents' interference, realize that you have the final decision about the person you marry and analyze objectively what your parents say about your choice. They may be right. If they are, do not be too proud to admit it. On the other hand, if your parents are wrong, you should decide the importance of maintaining the relationship with your partner. You may be forced to choose between your partner and your parents. If you value your partner over your parents and feel that your parents have been unjust in their accusations toward your partner, you may choose to marry your partner even though you may never see your parents again. This question may become, "Is my partner worth giving up the relationship with my parents?" He may be. He may not be. Either way, you will experience the impact for your decision.

Before making a decision, collect information. Look at the facts. If your parents want you to marry someone of the same religion or social class, rather than label them as snobs or bigots, take time to read some of the literature on mixed and cross-class marriages. You will find that those people who marry outside their religion and across social class lines have a higher divorce rate than those who marry someone of their own religion and/or social class (Landis and Landis, 1973). This does not imply that you should categorically not marry someone outside your religion or social class. It does raise the question of the advisability of doing so, however, and shifts the issue from the rebellion against your parents to whether or not this marriage at this time, to this person, is best.

SUMMARY

Effective communication is a prerequisite to developing an enjoyable relationship with your partner. Using a rating scale to express the intensity of your desires, asking honest questions, asking direct questions, and answering honestly your partner's questions (hopefully honest and direct), will help to prevent unnecessary misunderstandings in your relationship.

Jealous behavior can destroy a relationship. Its causes and expressions should be stopped and replaced by trusting behavior.

Confessing the past requires careful consideration. What should be told and to whom are decisions which should be made before blurting out one's confessions about the past.

Effective communication with your parents may be difficult. The bases for understanding each other are two different sets of experiences. You and your parents only know the world as you experience it. Differences of opinion are differences in learning experiences.

Where a conflict occurs over whom to marry, it is important to separate the issue of "should" from "can." You can marry whomever you choose. The better question is "should you?"

STUDY QUESTIONS

1. Explain the statement, "Communication means more than talking."
2. Give an example of how you can express your desires clearly.
3. Define and give an example of honest, dishonest, direct, and indirect questions.
4. How may your expression of jealous statements be reinforced by your partner?
5. Discuss the effect of jealous statements in regard to the Pygmalion effect.
6. What can you do to encourage your partner to be less jealous of your behavior?
7. What issues should you consider before talking about the past to your partner?
8. Why is communication with parents potentially difficult?
9. Give three reasons to explain why your parents try to discourage you from dating someone they do not like.
10. What are some guidelines to cope with your parents' interference in your relationship with your partner?

BIBLIOGRAPHY

CLARKE, C. Group procedures for increasing positive feedback between married couples. *The Family Coordinator,* 1970, **19,** 324–28.

HICKMAN, M. and BALDWIN, B. Use of programmed instruction to improve communication in marriage. *The Family Coordinator,* 1971, **20,** 121–25.

HINKLE, J. and MOORE, M. A student couples program. *The Family Coordinator,* 1971, **20,** 153–58.

LANDIS, J. and LANDIS, M. *Building a successful marriage,* 6th edition. Englewood Cliffs, New Jersey: Prentice-Hall, Inc., 1973.

PIERCE, R. Training in interpersonal communication skills with the partners of deteriorated marriages. *The Family Coordinator,* 1973, **22,** 223–27.

RAPPAPORT, A. The effects of an intensive conjugal relationship modification program. Unpublished doctoral dissertation, The Pennsylvania State University, 1971.

SATIR, V. *Conjoint family therapy.* Palo Alto, California: Science and Behavior Books, 1967.

STEINER, G. Parent-teen education: An exercise in communication. *The Family Coordinator,* 1970, **19,** 213–18.

WAKE, F. Attitudes of parents toward pre-marital sexual behavior of children and themselves. *Journal of Sexual Research,* 1969, **5,** #3.

Conclusion

This book has been concerned with four major issues: understanding yourself and the person with whom you become involved; selecting the interpersonal style compatible with your needs (marrying, living together, or remaining single); reviewing your reasons for marital commitment; and developing the skills for enriching an intimate interpersonal relationship.

Looking past the love feelings stirring in your relationship is a prerequisite for assessing your and your partner's self-concept, values, philosophy of life, goals, parents, education, and role compatibility. The theories of homogamy, complementary needs, and exchange are helpful in understanding the initiation and progress of your relationship.

After viewing your relationship in perspective, consider whether marrying, living together, or remaining single is your style.

An understanding of your reason for marriage should precede a decision to do so. Although love is the most frequent individual motivation for marriage, people marry for reasons of pregnancy, rebellion, escape, and physical appearance.

Regardless of your motivation to marry, the continuation of an enjoyable relationship is dependent on the appropriate use of sociological and psychological principles. These principles can be used to reduce conflict and resolve specific problems (interpersonal and sexual).

The result of carefully considering the central issues of marriage (who? when? and why?) is to increase the probability of making accurate decisions regarding your interpersonal happiness. Such decisions, when implemented, help to insure a better than even chance for interpersonal fulfillment.

APPENDIXES

Students enrolled in a marriage course often ask for specific guidelines to learn more about their relationships with their respective partners. Other students want to develop a greater understanding of how other people feel about marriage and the family. Still others want suggestions to resolve specific sexual problems. To meet the first two requests, two projects are presented. Appendix A, Assessing Your Relationship, details how two involved partners may learn more about each other. The second project, Appendix B, Experiencing Other People, suggests several interviews with different people to assess their thoughts about life, love, and marriage. The third request is taken up in Appendix C, Resolving Sexual Problems, which discusses four specific problems and provides procedures to overcome them.

A

Assessing Your Relationship

Bossard and Boll (1950) indicated that mate selection practices in America do not provide enough sobering, ceremonial features and that couples are allowed to drift into marriage with few preparatory rituals. The emphasis on romantic love may encourage you to make one of the most significant decisions of your life while under its hypnotic effect. This section of the Appendix suggests that you and your partner complete a project (Knox and Knox, 1974) designed to assist you in learning more about your relationship. This project was completed by 100 involved couples enrolled in marriage courses at East Carolina University. Their reaction to the project and the revision based on their evaluation, follow.

WHAT STUDENTS DID

Among other reasons, a marriage partner is selected on the basis of what he thinks (his beliefs, values) and does (his behavior). Twenty-four males and 76 females who defined themselves as "involved," gave information to and received information from their partners in the areas of economics, religion, children, sex, and a miscellaneous category involving information about in-laws, alcohol, and recreation. In addition to sharing opinions, the students took a hike, developed a budget, went to church, and visited their future in-laws with their partner.

MOST HELPFUL PART

After completing the project, students were asked, "What was the most meaningful part of the project?" Fifty-two percent of the students selected opinions; 35 percent, money; 6 percent, recreation; 5 percent, in-laws and 2 percent, religion as the most meaningful part of the project. The selections were *not* significantly related to sex, age, education, religion, marital relationships of parents, presence or absence of siblings, age at first date, age first "went steady," or number of months student had been involved with partner. In addition, each student evaluated each portion of the project in regard to: (1) whether or not it should be continued for future students, (2) whether or not it assisted him in learning more about his partner, and (3) whether or not it changed his feelings for his partner. The evaluation of each section follows.

Opinions

Ninety-eight percent of the students suggested that this part of the project be continued and over three-fourths said that they learned more about their partner from this experience. Over 40 percent said that their relationship had improved.

In the opinions section, each student was asked to anticipate how his partner would respond to 49 questions in regard to economics, children, religion, sex, and a miscellaneous category. After the partner responded to the 49 items, the student enrolled in the course noted discrepancies between what he thought his partner believed and what his partner actually believed.

The percent of discrepancies (percent of the total items in each section of opinions on which the student and partner disagreed) ranged from 16 percent in the area of sex to 10 percent in the area of economics. The miscellaneous category (14 percent), religion (13 percent) and children (12 percent) were between the extremes. The opinions section demonstrates that some "involved" students did not know as much about the beliefs of their partner as they thought they did.

Examples of disagreements and how they were resolved follow:

Carol feels that pre-marital sex is not right, while I think that the couple involved must decide this for themselves. Our compromise: No pre-marital sex.

In the area of contraception, Mary Ann believes in the rhythm method and I feel that a reliable form of birth control should be used until we are ready for children. No resolution.

What do you think a couple should do if there is an unexpected pregnancy before marriage? Mike believed the noble thing would be to get married. I thought he would say that, but I think an abortion is the best answer. Mike finally agreed with me, after I pointed out the many disadvantages of starting a marriage with an unexpected child.

If your husband (wife) should have an extra-marital affair, what would you do? Bill said he would seek a divorce and I said I would want a trial separation. We didn't resolve this because he wouldn't change his opinion and I think I would do what I choose.

What closely resembles your definition of religion? John replied "belief in the supreme being" and I said "a feeling you have within yourself." We haven't resolved this yet.

Sam thinks we should visit our parents more often than I do. We didn't resolve this issue, and I think it may cause some problems after we are married.

How much money will a wife make each month? He replied "$400 or below" and I replied "$500." I looked at him, sighed, and knowing the male ego, I didn't pursue the question any further.

I feel that the husband should manage the family money and Karen feels that this should be a joint affair.

I was always taught to give a tithe to church. Bob does not believe in this; he wants to give whatever he feels like giving. We talked about it; I told him how I felt and why I felt that way. Bob understood and agreed that we should give ten percent to the church, but he refused to give any to charities.

We also disagreed on having liquor in the house. Both my brother and I are allowed an occasional drink in the house. Barry drinks at my house also, but does not at his own. We decided that we would not drink around the children.

Landis and Landis (1973) studied 581 married couples to ascertain when they became aware of differences of opinion. Over 94 percent reported an awareness of differences over sex and children *after* marriage. Over 85 percent reported an awareness of a different perspective on money matters after they had tied the marital knot. Forty-one percent became aware of religious differences after marriage. The Landis data firmly support the position of the current study that students often drift through courtship talking about their classes, the latest *Playboy*, hit tune, or movie to the exclusion of their thoughts and feelings about central issues of their relationship and marriage. Once you are aware of how your partner feels about certain issues in regard to children, sex, money, and religion, you can decide whether or not you choose to commit yourself to this person for the rest of your life. This knowledge before marriage may help to avoid your discovering great discrepancies in thought and values after marriage. To terminate a relationship before marriage at its worst is called a "broken engagement"; after marriage, it is called a divorce.

The revised project which begins on page 182, encourages you to ask your partner specific questions in several areas of marital interaction. In addition, you are encouraged to provide specific information for your partner which will allow each of you to better evaluate the other.

Money

Aside from the opinions section, money was evaluated as the most informative part of the project. Each partner developed one budget showing how he thought the available income should be spent for rent, food, entertainment, insurance, etc., and another budget noting how he thought his partner would allocate the money. The discrepancies were observed and a final budget developed. In addition, the couple selected an apartment and furniture for the apartment. These experiences were designed to bring out any differences in regard to how their income should be spent.

Ninety-five percent of the respondents suggested that the money section of the project be continued for future students and over 75 percent noted they learned more about their partners. Feelings toward the partner were unchanged (67 percent) or improved (30 percent). Verbatim evaluations of this section follow:

This section made us both realize that we do not actually know as much as we should concerning such things as life insurance, car payments, etc. It is useful as a stimulus to learn of these prices.

This section helped me to learn about her naiveté concerning the cost of certain commodities.

Although money was always considered a "problem area" for us, we had never discussed actual facts and figures. Now that he has a permanent job, we had some real figures to work with and sat down and discussed how and where our money would be spent.

I learned that Gary is concerned about being able to provide for me, and that he respects what I think when it comes to money. So many men think women are "no-minds" in this area.

I learned that his tastes are a little different from mine and we may have some conflict when we go shopping for a home.

This section was important because I became increasingly aware that marriage is a great financial burden. Whereas one's responsibility, while single, is only to himself and to a lesser degree toward others; when married, the responsibility toward one's spouse, and the ever-present need for money, demonstrate the need for a carefully planned and organized budget before marriage. Naturally, an adequate income should be established prior to marriage.

One student who did not benefit from this section said:

The money part of this project should be revised for future students. First of all, if a couple is getting married soon, as assumed in the project, they would have discussed money at length beforehand. Devising three budgets is a waste of time. An accurate budget cannot be devised until after marriage and in the real situation. There are too many outside factors that vary, such as electricity costs, etc.

Out of 164 divorced people studied by Landis and Landis (1973), over half reported that they "almost always disagreed about money." Differences over money may create feelings of hostility and frustration for two reasons:

(1) Money becomes valuable to people because it takes time to obtain it. If you have been employed during the summer or part-time during the school year, you know that workers are frequently paid in proportion to the amount of time they spend engaging in a particular activity. It probably took you a long time to accumulate the money that you received. The money has become valuable to you because of the time it took to earn it. This is particularly true if you did not enjoy what you were doing to earn the money.

(2) Disagreement over how money should be spent feeds from the issue of the amount of time it takes to get money. Specifically, although our culture teaches us that material possessions are desirable, it does not specify

which ones are desirable. What you define as attractive and necessary, your partner may regard as ugly and useless. Hence, knowing your partner's economic values prior to marriage will allow you to: (a) decide that the differences are not important, (b) completely change your values and/or behaviors, (c) compromise your values and/or behaviors with those of your partner, or (d) terminate the relationship and identify someone who shares your economic values. Although terminating the relationship may appear to be a poor alternative, couples who do not resolve their differences, keep them. This was demonstrated by LeMasters (1959) who noted that some couples continued to have the same problem throughout a ten-year period. It is unwise to pretend that "something" will happen to resolve your differences in the area of money unless you actively engage in one of the above conflict reducing alternatives.

In-Laws

For the in-law section of the project, the partners visited in each other's homes for a week-end. During their stay, they observed the interaction between their future in-laws. Specifically, they recorded the number of positive and negative statements each in-law made to the other. The purpose of this was to provide specific information with regard to how the parents of the prospective mate interact with each other, and to note in what ways the prospective mate acts the same toward his or her partner as the same sex parent (of the prospective mate) acts toward the opposite sex parent. For example, does John act toward Sally (his girlfriend) the same way John's father acts toward John's mother? Likewise, does Sally act toward John the same way Sally's mother acts toward her father? Finally, each partner observed the relationship between his own father and mother in regard to the dominant partner and noted the effect this relationship had on the way he behaved toward his date.

Over three-fourths of the respondents thought this section should be continued. Only 40 percent reported that they learned more about their partner, however, while 75 percent said their relationship was unchanged. Examples of reactions to this section follow:

> Most people are products of their environments, and watching their parents is the most direct way of understanding why and how your partner reacts to both you and the outside world. Also, I have noticed how affected I am by his opinions about my parents.

> I really think it was a bit premature in our relationship to start considering in-laws. I do not believe this should be a part of the project—to journey to the prospective in-law's house and take data.

It is important that every involved couple meet the future in-laws, although I feel this part could be changed to be more useful. To me it would have been more useful if we would have told about experiences we shared with our parents or things we did together rather than writing down positive and negative statements.

I did not learn anything new about Boomer; only why he is the way he is. Viewing him in his home situation allowed me to understand him better. I was able to see how his parents influenced him.

Religion

Next to the section on recreation, this section was evaluated as least helpful. Students visited in each other's church or in a third church which they might mutually choose. Almost one-fourth of the respondents suggested that this section be discontinued, over half said they did not learn anything new about their partner, and only 13 percent said it had a positive effect on their relationship. Landis and Landis (1973) also observed that most couples (59 percent) seemed to have worked out their religious differences before marriage.

Reactions to this section included:

We both realize religion is a poor topic of conversation, but we feel it is nothing that can't be solved. He resented going to a Protestant church just because he resented "being made," as he said it, to go to church. We realize some decision will have to be made, but prefer not to start arguing about it 1½ years before we marry. We already knew each other's views about religion so this part only served as a sore point for us.

This section should be optional. I say this because religion is not as important to today's young couples as it was a generation ago.

We both felt strongly that the religious section should not be continued. We were forced into doing something that we don't believe in. After both having such a negative reaction to the sermon, it tended to bring us closer in our agreement. We learned we felt the same way in this respect.

Recreation

The involved couples each took a four-mile hike around the university campus in an attempt to reduce inhibitions and to let the partner see how the other would behave under conditions of physical stress. The couples evaluated the hike as being the most useless aspect of the project.

Almost one-third (31.8 percent) of the students suggested the hike be discontinued for future students, over two-thirds (69.6 percent) noted that they did not learn more about their partner, and over four-fifths (83.15 percent) said that their feelings for their partner had not changed as a function of the hike.

A junior coed who has been dating her partner for over a year remarked:

> This part of the project should definitely be discontinued. It was very foolish and proved nothing. The *only* thing I learned is how fast I could walk. I expected it to take much longer. This did not change any of my feelings; only that I was surprised my partner did it. If the situation had been reversed, I know I would not have done all this busy work for a course I was not taking.

However, representing those who indicated the recreation portion of the project should be continued, two students wrote:

> Randy and I had fun on the hike but it did not necessarily help us to learn more about each other. My feelings about Randy grew stronger in a way. The hike somehow generated an atmosphere of closeness and warmth even though it was a cold winter's day.

> The most meaningful part of the project was the hike because we were alone and we talked a lot about different things.

Revision

On the basis of student evaluation, the project was revised. The new directions allow you and your partner to select those parts of the project which will be meaningful to you at this time in your relationship. The probability of the project having a negative effect on your relationship is minimal. Just over one percent evaluated the project as making their relationship worse. On the other hand, one couple, anxious to explain the positive influence the project had on their relationship, noted "We got married."

PROJECT FOR "INVOLVED"

If you are living together (or thinking of doing so) or considering marrying someone who lives within a 200-mile radius of your campus, you may complete selected portions of this project for which you can earn credit as specified by your instructor.

The project is designed to help you learn more about your partner and your relationship. It is divided into two parts. Part I, Opinions on Marriage, is concerned with clarifying for you what your partner believes about economics, religion, children, sex, in-laws, alcohol, and recreation. In the same way, your beliefs will be clarified for your partner. Complete this section.

Part II, Thinking and Doing Together, may involve your taking a hike together (recreation), developing a budget, selecting an apartment or furniture (money), attending church (religion), or visiting each other's parents (in-laws). Select and complete those sections which will be meaningful to you and your partner at this time in your relationship. Your teacher will give you additional credit for more work. The purpose of these exercises is to share a number of varied experiences together and to observe your partner's behaviors in a number of different situations.

The project is due on _____. Please type your project; it will be returned to you at the end of the term.

SCRAPBOOK FORMAT DIRECTIONS

Please read these directions carefully. You are responsible for reporting your experiences as specified.

Title Page:
OUR SCRAPBOOK, Today's date
Title and number of course
Your name
Your partner's name

Table of Contents: List the items you have placed in your scrapbook; give the page numbers.

Part   I.   Opinions on Marriage
  A.   Place the answers to the questions entitled Opinions on Marriage in your scrapbook.
  B.   On what specific points did you disagree? How were these resolved?
Part   II.   Thinking and Doing Together (report those you selected)
  A.   Recreation
    1.   List the day and time you took the hike together. State the amount of time it took you to complete the hike.
  B.   Money
    1.   Present the information asked for in section I, II, III, IV, or V under "Money." Identify them as follows: I—My Budget, II—His Budget, III—Our Budget, IV—Apartment, V—Furniture.

   C. Religion
    1. Identify which option you selected (I, II, or III) and present the information requested in *a* through *c* under I in the section on Religion.
   D. In-Laws
    1. Provide the information requested in *a* through *i* under In-Laws.
  Part III. Evaluation
    Turn in separately and anonymously.
    Please be frank.
    1. What was the most meaningful portion of the project for you (Opinions, Recreation, Money, Religion, or In-Laws)? Why?
    2. Evaluate each section that you completed of Part II (Opinions, Recreation, Money, Religion, and In-Laws) in regard to *each* of the following:
     a. Did this part of the project help you learn more about your partner? If so, in what way?
     b. In what way, if any, have your feelings changed about your partner as a result of this part of the project?

PART I
OPINIONS ON MARRIAGE

Assume that you plan to be married in one month. Ask your partner the following questions. Write down his (her) answers. Have your partner ask you the same questions and have him (her) write down your answers.

ECONOMICS—Information potential wife should find out from potential husband.

1. What kind of job will you have? Where will we live? How much will your job require that you travel? How often will we be moving because of your job?

2. How much money will you make the first year we are married?

3. How much of your net income do you believe in giving to church or charity?

4. Whom do you want to manage the money?

5. When we disagree over whether or not we should buy something, who should make the final decision?

6. Will we have a separate or joint bank account?

7. How much money will we each have each week to spend?

8. Suppose I wanted a full time career, how would you feel about that?

9. How often will you want to go on vacation? How much per year should be spent on vacation?

10. How will we travel on vacation—bus, car, plane, train?

11. How much money will you expect me to make out first year of marriage?

12. What is your parents' annual income?

13. How much money do you think we should save monthly?

14. Do you want me to account to you for the money I spend?

Information potential husband should find out from potential wife.

1. Do you want to work? Elaborate. Do you see that your primary role is that of wife and mother or are you more interested in some type of job or career? How will the money you make be spent?

2. What is your attitude toward my job? Would you choose to have the same job? Why or why not?

3. Same as questions 2, 3, 4, 5, 6, 7, 9, 10, 11, 12, 13, and 14 above.

RELIGION AND CHILDREN—Information potential wife should find out from potential husband and vice versa.

1. What do you think about religion, God, prayer, life after death, the concept of a "Christian (or Jewish) home"? Elaborate on each of these.

2. Do you go to religious services? Where? How often? Do you pray? How often? What do you pray about? When we are married, how often would you choose to go to church or synagogue? Do you want your children to be reared in your religion?

3. How do you feel about abortion?

4. What do you think about children? Do you want them? Why? How many? Why? When? Why? At what intervals? Why? How will you provide "sex education" for your children?

5. Suppose I did not want to have children; how would you feel? What would you do?

6. To your knowledge, can you have children?

7. Do you want your children to go to public or private schools?

8. Who should discipline the children? How?

SEX—Information potential wife should find out from potential husband.

1. Do you believe in premarital intercourse? Why? If not, how much sexual intimacy do you think is appropriate? Be specific.

2. What do you think about oral sex? Masturbation?

3. What type of contraception do you suggest? Why? Suppose that method did not work?

4. What are your values about sex outside of marriage? Suppose I were to have an affair and later told you; what would you do? Why?

5. How much foreplay do you like? What kind of foreplay do you like? Be specific.

6. What do you think a couple should do if there is an unexpected pregnancy before marriage?

7. If we had problems achieving sexual or marital adjustment, would you agree to see a marriage counselor?

8. Suppose I didn't like sex, what would you do?

Information potential husband should find out from potential wife.

1–8. Same as above.

9. Are your menstrual periods regular?

10. Do you experience any discomfort related to menstruation?

11. Have you experienced what you define to be an orgasm?

OTHER QUESTIONS—To be answered by both.

1. Who do you think should have the most power in making family decisions?

2. When will we be able to afford a color TV, stereo, and home?

3. Where are some places that you would like to spend vacations?

4. Which sport would you like most to learn and participate in? Why?

5. How much should each mate contribute in cleaning the apartment, preparing the meals, doing the laundry, etc? What specifically are you willing to do in each of these areas?

6. What one behavior do you want me to do to please you more often?

7. What do you want me to say or not to say to make you happier?

8. What do you think of yourself? Describe yourself.

9. Do you drink booze and smoke pot? If so, how much? Have you experienced hard drugs?

10. Will we have liquor and/or pot in our apartment or home? Why?

11. Suppose I died; would you marry again? Why?

12. Suppose you died; would you want me to marry again? Why?

13. Suppose we couldn't get along; would you be willing to get a divorce?

14. Do you think I get jealous easily? How will you cope with my jealousy.

15. Do you love me? Why?

16. What does love mean to you?

17. What do you want out of life? What are your goals?

18. What is your relationship with your parents?

19. What do you like and dislike about my parents?

20. Will we live near your parents, or mine, or both? What do you think about my mother living with us?

21. When we are married, how many evenings will you want to spend away from the apartment without me?

22. How do your parents get along? Rate their marriage on a 0-10 scale (0 = unhappy; 10 = happy). Describe their marriage in terms of role responsibilities.

To prepare this information for your scrapbook, number the questions, copy the questions, and then write the answers to the questions. If either you or your partner feel that a question is such that you do not want to write the answer, say that you don't feel comfortable writing the answer but that you have ascertained the information. Since the nature of your answers may be very personal, only your instructor will read it.

PART II.
THINKING AND DOING TOGETHER (select at least two)

A. RECREATION. Take a four-mile hike with your partner. Leave at 6:00 a.m. Do not eat breakfast before going and take only enough lunch for one person.
   Other directions include:

a. Go alone. If another couple is hiking too, wait until they are far enough ahead of you so that you cannot see them before you begin.
b. Hold hands with each other the entire trip. Always walk on the left side of the highway, facing traffic.
c. Leave a note with your instructor at least 2 days before you and your partner plan to take the hike. (Your instructor may ride by to confirm that you are making the trip.)
   1. Specify who is taking the trip (your name and your date's name).
   2. Specify the day and time you will leave, and from what point going where.
   3. Specify your clothing. (As an example, girl will wear red blouse and blue pants; boy will wear green shirt and black pants.)

B. MONEY. (Complete I, II, III or IV or V)

I. Develop a budget without consulting your date: (1) Estimate the amount of money monthly the two of you will have to spend. (2) Specify how much money is to be spent monthly on each of the following: (a) rent, (b) utilities (heating, air conditioning, lights, water, sewage disposal), (c) telephone, (d) food, (e) transportation (car—gas, oil, tires, insurance; bus; other); (f) life insurance, (g) health insurance, and (h) entertainment (movies, records, tapes, beer, pot, trips to beach, etc.).
II. Have your date perform 1 and 2 above without consulting you.
III. Observe the discrepancies (if any) in regard to your independent decisions as to how the money should be spent and develop a budget together (specify how the money that will be available to you is to be spent when you are married.)
IV. Select an apartment together that you would live in after you are married. Observe at least three apartments before deciding. In reporting this experience, provide the following information: (a) Names of the apartments about which you inquired, (b) names and phone numbers of the apartment managers with whom you talked, (c) name of the apartment you

selected and a description of the living room, kitchen, and bedroom, and (d) rent, approximate monthly utilities, and terms of contract (12 months or month-to-month) for the apartment you selected.

V. Go together to one of the several furniture stores in your area. Select independently a sofa, coffee table, end tables, and two lamps that you would buy for your apartment. In reporting this experience, provide the following information: (a) Describe and list the price of the sofa, coffee table, end tables, and lamps that you liked and that your date liked, (b) describe [if different] the sofa, coffee table, end tables, and lamps that the two of you finally decided to buy, (c) specify when and where you selected this furniture, (d) specify the name and telephone number of the person who helped you in the furniture showroom.

C. RELIGION (Complete I or II or III)

I. If neither you nor your date has an interest in organized religion (define yourself as an atheist or agnostic), identify a church or synagogue which most closely approximates your beliefs and attend. In reporting this experience, provide the following information:

   a. name and date you attended church or synagogue.

   b. church or synagogue bulletin.

   c. summary of the "sermon" (each summarize independently)

   d. critique of the "sermon" (write the critical analysis separately)

   e. each partner write his impressions of the date's critical analysis of the sermon.

II. If you and your date belong to different churches (you are Baptist, he is Methodist) or different religions (one Catholic, one Protestant), go together to each other's church on two separate Sundays (Saturday if Jewish). After you have attended each worship service, complete items *a* through *e* under section I.

III. If you and your date belong to the same church (synagogue), identify a church of your denomination that neither of you has attended before. Attend this church and complete items *a* through *e* under section I.

D. IN-LAWS. Visit your possible future in-laws with your date for a week-end. Ask your date to visit you in your home for a week-end. Provide the following information for *each* visit.

   a. Names and addresses of in-laws visited.

   b. Number of times you have visited in the home of your possible future in-laws previously.

   c. Number of times your date has visited in your home previously.

   d. Nature and number of positive statements your potential mother-in-law made to your potential father-in-law. Example: When Mrs. Jones says to Mr. Jones, "Thank you," "The Smith's are nice people," or "That was a good sermon," write down the statement, and keep a record of how many positive statements she makes.

e. Nature and number of positive statements your potential father-in-law made to your potential mother-in-law.

f. Nature and number of negative statements your potential mother-in-law made to your potential father-in-law. Example: When Mrs. Jones says to Mr. Jones, "What a terrible day it is," "You are always late," "Can't you ever do anything right," write down the statement and keep a record of how many negative statements she makes.

g. Nature and number of negative statements your potential father-in-law made to your potential mother-in-law.

h. Describe the relationship between your mother and your father. Who is the dominant partner in your parents' marriage? Who is the dominant partner in the relationship with your date? In what ways do you behave toward your date as does your same sex parent behave toward the opposite sex parent?

i. Both you and your date should complete separately the information required.

If it is not possible to visit your future in-laws (residence outside 200-mile radius, in-laws deceased, etc.), complete only *h* of this section.

BIBLIOGRAPHY

BOSSARD, J. H. and BOLL, E. S. *Ritual in Family Living.* Philadelphia: University of Pennsylvania Press, 1950.

GOODMAN, L. A. Modifications of the Dorn-Stouffer-Tibbitts method for testing the significance of comparisons in sociological data. *American Journal of Sociology,* January, 1961, 355–59.

KNOX, D. and PATRICK, J. You are what you do: A new approach in preparation for marriage. *The Family Coordinator,* April, 1971, 109–14.

KNOX, D. and KNOX, F. Preparation for marriage: Beyond the classroom. *Journal of Family Counseling,* 1974, in press.

LANDIS, J. and LANDIS, M. *Building a Successful Marriage,* 6th edition. Englewood Cliffs, New Jersey: Prentice-Hall, Inc., 1973.

LEMASTERS, E. E. Holy deadlock: A study of unsuccessful marriages. *The Midwest Sociologist,* July, 1959, 86–91.

B

Experiencing Other People

WHAT?

The purpose of this project is to find out how other people experience various social roles and how they view marriage and the family. The procedure involves interviewing males and females at various stages of the family life cycle, and those who do not conveniently fit into the cycle.

WHO? (Select 10)

1. Engaged
2. Early marriage, 1–3 years (no children)
3. Young children in marriage (oldest child under 30 months)
4. School-age children in marriage (oldest child 6–12 years)
5. Teenagers in marriage (oldest child 13–20 years)

6. Retired
7. Divorced
8. Widowed
9. Parent of a retarded child
10. Single, career woman (over 40)
11. Two-career couple (no children)
12. Two-career couple (children)
13. Childless couple (over 50)
14. Lesbian
15. Homosexual
16. Couple living together with no legal contract
17. Alcoholic
18. Remarried (one partner married before)
19. Separated (one partner away for at least one year—e.g., military absence)
20. Couple married for 50 years.
21. Married couple in which age difference is 10 years or more.
22. Interracial marriage.
23. Married couple with adopted child.
24. Spouse who has in-law living in home.
25. Spouses who have reversed traditional roles (husband takes care of children, wife works).
26. Other unusual situation.

The people you interview should be virtually strangers to you. Ask people you know to arrange an interview for you with someone they know. Half the people you interview should be male; the other half female.

HOW?

Introduce yourself to the person you would like to interview. You might say that you are taking a course in marriage and that you have been asked to interview various people. Ask the person if he (she) is willing to share his (her) views with you. Most will be delighted to do so.

After you have the person's consent, your job is to get inside that person's head and crawl around. Ask about 10 open-ended questions. For example, "How do you feel about premarital sex?" rather than "Do you think premarital sex is wrong?"; "How did you feel when your fiancée broke the engagement?" rather than "Did you feel hurt when your engagement was broken?" In other words, avoid questions that can be answered "yes," or "no." Examples of closed-ended questions are: "Are you sorry about the way things turned out?" and "Do you think living together is wrong?"

Write-up

Begin each interview on a new page.

1. Write a description of each person you interviewed. (Into which of the 26 suggested categories does he [she] fall; age, education, etc.)
2. List and number the questions you asked and their answers. (Question #1, answer. Question #2, answer, etc.)
3. Write your impressions of each person (happy, depressed, ambivalent, bland).
4. Write your response to each person's answers (truthful, cynical, defensive).
5. What was the most striking thing each person said to you in each of your interviews? (One statement or response from each person.)
6. You may record one through five on cassette tapes instead of writing everything out. The tapes will not be returned to you.

Evaluation

Turn in separately and anonymously.

1. What was the most meaningful aspect of this project?
2. Do you think you received more accurate information from strangers or friends?
3. What specific changes should be made to improve the project?

EXAMPLE OF INTERVIEW

The following is the verbatim interview of a married woman with a young child.

Description: Mrs. Z is a college graduate. She has been married for 3 years and has one child. As far as her background is concerned, I don't really know because she was a total stranger to me prior to the interview.

Questions and Answers

1. How many times daily does your mate say "I love you"? How many times daily do you tell your mate that you love him?

My husband usually tells me he loves me at least 3 to 5 times daily, but naturally more often in intimate circumstances. This increases during the weekend as we are together more often since I work and he goes to college during the weekdays. However, I do not feel that counting the number of times really has any meaning. Some people have a habit of saying "I love you" because it is expected, but in our case we tell one another "I love you" because we actually feel the need to let the other know it. Some people do not feel the need to say the words. Either way, the number of times the phrase itself is said is not a measure of one's love. Actually, it is the action that often speaks more loudly than the words. I would prefer to disregard my earlier statement of the number of times he says, "I love you" because when my husband does something that shows love, no matter how small that action might be, I feel he is actually speaking those words as well as acting them out—and these, I might add, are very often too numerous to count.

2. How do you feel about premarital sexual intercourse?

I feel very strongly about the appropriateness of premarital sexual intercourse for myself, but this does not mean that I suggest it for everyone. Some people, too many times, have guilt feelings later in life and this is wrong. My husband and I experienced this and for us it was not wrong because neither of us felt guilty (even after my parents knew that we had experienced this intimate relationship). One cannot, then, say it is right or wrong for any individual except one's self. There are too many people involved like family, etc., that can influence your thinking. I can only say that it was right for me, with no guilt feeling afterwards, and I shall never regret having had premarital sexual intercourse.

3. What do you consider to be the one biggest advantage of marriage?

I myself cannot depict one big advantage in marriage because I feel marriage is a combination of all of these needs and more that married people desire. It depends on what your need at a given time is as to what one might consider to be most important. If I feel a need for sex tonight, then my biggest advantage at that time is that I have my husband to fulfill this need. If I lose a loved one tomorrow, my biggest advantage at that time is that I have my husband to fulfill the need of strength to help me through that loss. If I feel lonely and depressed, I have the security of knowing that my husband will stand by me and help me realize that life is worth living and help bring me out of my depressed state. So to me there is no biggest advantage. It really depends on what your present needs are.

4. Do you believe in the old adage: "love conquers all"?

DEFINITELY NOT! Believe me, it takes a lot more than two people's love for one another to pay the rent, buy the food, clothe the baby, pay the utility, gas, telephone, life insurance, hospitalization insurance, car insurance, and doctors' bills. Love for one another provides the strength you need many times to get through these crises, but that's all it provides

—even though that is a great deal. I'm working to put my husband through school on the G.I. Bill. We have a 9-month-old baby. Believe me, we love her dearly, but our love surely won't buy her food. Our love helps me to keep going even though it seems we may never get ahead and that it is hopeless.

5. What do you feel is the role of a wife? Husband?

I don't feel marriage is a role. I do not feel there is any set of rules to go by as far as duties, etc., but rather these are interchangeable and flexible. My husband helps when he can and uses this as a means by which he is saying "I love you." The privileges are shared—there's not a dividing line to go by.

6. What do you consider to be the five qualities most important in a relationship to produce a happy and successful marriage?

This varies among people, but I feel they are important as follows:
a. I like my husband as well as love him.
b. I respect him and his opinions and feelings, although we do not always agree.
c. I trust him in his decisions as well as his faithfulness to me.
d. I listen to him and his problems and try not to belittle him for his failings.
e. I admire him for standing up for his beliefs and not letting people run over him when he feels he is right. Also, he takes pride in his accomplishments.

7. In your opinion, what is the major source of conflict between husbands and wives? What causes the most arguments?

Here again, I believe that there is no real major source of conflict except at a given time or circumstance. As a whole, however, I would say that if one area had to be chosen, it would be in-laws.

8. If you were unhappy with your marriage, would you seek professional counseling? If so, when?

Not unless all else had failed—and I mean after communication and discussion of problems between us, help from or discussion with our minister. We have often found very close friends a help, but most of the time we are able to discuss our problems and often resolve our problems ourselves with patience, love, and understanding. Sometimes it becomes heated and angry, but we always manage to find each other. If I really felt we were getting nowhere then I would seek professional counseling and would encourage my husband go with me.

9. Do you feel that children bring husband and wife even closer or have the opposite effect?

I feel an answer can only be made in our own circumstances, and I feel it has brought us closer together because our child was produced from love for each other and is now a human being. It has made us strive harder for a better life because we love our daughter so much.

10. Do you feel that success in marriage comes naturally to those who are in love or is it a goal that a couple must strive to achieve?

We love each other and always have, but our success has not come naturally. We have had to strive to make it work because I know there have been too many times when we could have much easier said "forget it" and given up because things began to get tough. I can only answer for ourselves, and I feel that it is something you must work toward and *never* take for granted because you can quickly learn that it is not something that will always be there because at any time something can go wrong and it takes a lot to pick up the pieces and put them back together again— but it's worth it for me!

Impression

Mrs. Z was amazingly frank especially since we were total strangers—or maybe for that reason. She was very definite in what she felt, and didn't mind stating her opinions. I personally agree with much of what she said. In her answer to the first question, she says that the things her husband does often show her that he loves her more clearly than if he said the words. This is related to what we learned about values. He shows her that he values *her* by doing things for her and with her, and tries doing with his time those things that please her. Also, I think her values were good (#6) when she states that she likes her husband as well as loves him. I really think she put more thought into these questions than any other person I interviewed since it took about two hours of discussion between us to come up with these responses. It is good that she challenges the questions because, by themselves, they *are* rather meaningless.

Most Striking Remark

I think the most striking thing said to me during this interview was Mrs. Z's opinion toward premarital intercourse. It sounded to me as if she was trying to justify her actions to herself or to me. I think she *did* have feelings of guilt despite what she said, mainly because she never said *why* she was glad she had premarital intercourse. She did not say that these experiences brought them closer, contributed to their relationship or anything else. If she could have cited a specific advantage, this would be different, but her attitude seemed rather defensive to me.

C

Resolving Sexual Problems [1]

Although some couples do not have intercourse before marriage, most do (Reiss, 1971) Sexual problems encountered by these couples are similar to those experienced by married couples. This section details four of these problems: disagreement over frequency of intercourse, lack of orgasm, impotence, and premature ejaculation. An explanation of the nature of each problem is followed by a procedure which has been helpful in resolving the problem.

FREQUENCY

Macklin (1972) observed that "differing degrees or periods of sexual interest" was the most frequent sexual problem reported by the students

---

[1] This section is adapted from portions of *Dr. Knox's Marital Exercise Book,* by David Knox, published by David McKay, Inc., forthcoming.

she studied who were living together. The problem occurs when one partner is refused while trying to initiate sexual behavior with the other. For example, the male will roll over in bed, kiss his partner on the cheek, and stroke her breasts or genitals in preparation for intercourse. She may push his hand away and slide her body from him. Both partners become angry. He is thinking, "What's the matter with her? She wasn't always this way. She tricked me." Her thoughts are, "Why doesn't he show me affection when we are out of bed? It seems as though he only gets close to me when he wants sex." Regardless of the facts, each partner feels and believes that his anger is justified and that his partner's behavior is unreasonable.

To resolve the problem, two things must occur: (1) each partner must communicate to the other that he understands why his partner feels the way he does; and (2) a plan must be developed and executed to resolve the disagreement. The female should understand that rejecting her partner for intercourse involves not only his loss of a pleasurable orgasmic experience but his feelings of personal rejection. The male should understand that sex and affection, for the female, are often separate. Hugging, holding, touching, and kissing in preparation for intercourse is not the same as these behaviors not followed by intercourse. The former encourages feelings in the female that the only interest her partner has is in her body, whereas the latter encourages the feeling that she is loved and wanted as a person.

After discussing these perspectives with each other, new behaviors should begin. Ultimately, the male would like his female to respond favorably to intercourse and feel free to initiate sexual interaction. The female would like her partner to hold her, kiss her, and be close to her without invariably following these behaviors with intercourse. Since each knows what the other wants, he should begin to engage in these behaviors.

To illustrate how difficulties over frequency of intercourse can be overcome, assume a male wants intercourse three times a week whereas his partner desires intercourse once a week. The following procedure has been helpful in overcoming differences in sexual desires:

1. The female should attempt to seduce her partner five times for intercourse during one week. She might start seducing him early in the day by telling him about the big night ahead.
2. The male should refuse to have intercourse the first two times she tries to seduce him. Under no circumstances should he give in regardless of how much he (or she) wants intercourse.
3. The male should refuse intercourse one of the remaining three times his partner tries to seduce him (intercourse will occur twice).
4. Most important, the male should hug and kiss his partner on two surprise occasions each day. These demonstrations of affection are never to be followed by intercourse.

Do not be hesitant to make these specific rules with your partner. The procedure has been effective for the problem described.

Using this procedure, a new attitude toward intercourse will develop for both partners. The female learns that her partner can give her affection (hugs and kisses) without intercourse occurring and that he does have the willpower to refuse intercourse even though she tries to seduce him. The male learns that his partner likes sex since she approaches him for intercourse.

Although, traditionally, husbands have complained that wives did not want intercourse as frequently as they, Bell (1967) observed that 25 percent of 196 college-educated females complained that intercourse was "too infrequent." When this is the case, that the female wants intercourse more frequently than her partner, the procedure suggested above can be changed so that the male is the agressor and the female refuses. One effect of her refusing to have intercourse is to increase his desire to have intercourse more frequently.

In general, the procedure calls for the partner with the less frequent desire for intercourse to seduce, several times in one week, the partner who wants frequent intercourse. The first two times, and occasionally thereafter, the partner should refuse intercourse. Meanwhile, the partner who wants frequent intercourse should hug and kiss his partner on two surprise occasions each day, but never follow these behaviors with intercourse.

NO ORGASM

Macklin (1972) noted that almost half of the Cornell undergraduate females living with their boyfriends listed lack of orgasm as a problem. Females who have not experienced climax may feel strange and abnormal in a society which proclaims orgasm as the ultimate achievement. A trim art major who had been living with her partner for six months said, "I haven't had one."

The capacity to have orgasm is influenced by your attitude toward sex, the relationship with your partner, and adequate physical stimulation. Some mothers encourage their daughters to believe that sex is shameful and dirty and that males are sexual beasts with questionable motives. These parental teachings are the result of: (1) parental acceptance of the truth of the beliefs; and (2) an attempt to scare the daughter into virginity. Although systematic indoctrination that sex is shameful may be effective in delaying intercourse until marriage, sexual adjustment in marriage may be marred. It is difficult to establish positive attitudes toward sex in marriage after 15–20 years of negative sexual training.

If you have been taught that sex is dirty and shameful, three behaviors will assist you in developing a more positive attitude toward your own sexuality. First, identify one of your female friends whom you feel has a positive attitude toward sex and encourage her to tell you about its delights. If she, too, has a negative set for sex, ask another friend. The objective is to talk with someone you admire, trust and respect who has a positive attitude toward sex. Second, read a book like *The Sensuous Woman* ("J," 1969) which encourages you to develop positive attitudes about sex. You might also consider seeing a film which shows some of the sexually explicit materials about which you have been reading. If you are "turned off" by your reading or viewing, do not force yourself. Continue to talk with your friend about her positive attitude toward sex until you become curious to learn more.

Third, masturbation will help you experience pleasurable sexual feelings. Take time with yourself. Allow about an hour and a half. Select a time when you believe no one will knock on your door. If you have a phone, take it off the hook. Begin by taking a warm bath. Wash yourself with your hands (not a wash cloth). Rub your moist, soapy, hands and fingers over your breasts and genitals. Do this as long as you feel comfortable doing so. If you begin to get anxious, stop. If you are unable to touch yourself, consult a marriage counselor or psychologist who will assist you in reducing your anxiety.

Assuming that you enjoyed the bathtub exercise, dry off and lay nude on the bed. Place a mirror between your legs and observe your genitals. A basic anatomy book will be helpful in identifying the parts of your genitalia.

After you have acquainted yourself with your genitalia, stroke your vaginal area with the palm of your hand and fingers. After several minutes you may begin to experience a sensation which you define as pleasurable. Continue to stroke your genitals. Identify the correct place, pressure, and rhythm which excites you most. In regard to place, most females report pleasurable sensations from rubbing their fingers along the shaft of the clitoris. Other females enjoy inserting a finger in the vagina and moving it across the clitoris. In regard to pressure, some enjoy an almost crushing movement while others enjoy a soft, feather-like touch. In regard to rhythm, some enjoy the quickness of a street drill while others enjoy a slow, violin movement.

These masturbatory exercises should be practiced over a period of weeks and months. Do not expect an orgasm the first several times you try these exercises. Do expect an increasing amount of pleasure and a positive change in your attitude toward sex.

Another method of self-stimulation is by using an electric vibrator.

These are sold in large drugstores as massagers. When placed over the vaginal area, the vibratory sensations often produce extremely pleasurable feelings within just a few minutes.

Should you choose to use the vibrator, keep three things in mind: (1) Make certain that you are relaxed and that you have had plenty of sleep that day. In other words, you should feel physically healthy. (2) Be prepared to move the vibrator from place to place over your vagina to discover where it feels best. Some women report that they experience pain while using the vibrator. This usually results from the vibrator being held directly over the clitoris. Removing the vibrator from the place of pain will be followed by more pleasurable sensations. (3) Be patient. The vibrator will not produce a climax every time. Every time you masturbate manually or by using the vibrator, you should have a "maybe so-maybe not" attitude toward an orgasm occurring that particular time. If you demand that an orgasm occur, it probably will not.

To this point, we have discussed achieving orgasm without a partner. You may choose to experience orgasm through heavy petting (but not intercourse) or through intercourse itself. In either case, it may be important that you are involved in a deep emotional mutual commitment with your partner. Traditionally, females have been socialized to experience sex within a context of love. Although heavy petting on the first date may be unacceptable, that same behavior during engagement may be expected by both partners.

Assuming that you are involved in a relationship at the level you feel is appropriate and assuming that you want to experience orgasm through manual stimulation, your task is to teach your partner what you have already learned about yourself. Through masturbation, you have identified the place, pressure, and rhythm which results in pleasurable sexual feelings for you. Making the touch-and-ask rule with your partner will help him to learn how to excite you. The rule states, "Every time you touch your partner, ask your partner how it feels." In this way, your partner can get direct feedback about his effect on you and can learn what you like best. By his following your directions, you can teach him to bring you to an enjoyable orgasm.

If you have decided to have intercourse, you may be concerned about lack of orgasm during intercourse even though you can achieve a climax through manual stimulation. To accomplish orgasm during intercourse once you have mastered orgasm through manual stimulation, have your partner manually stimulate you to the point of orgasm. After you have begun your orgasmic spin, ask him to penetrate. The purpose of this procedure is to associate the penis with orgasm.

After practicing this procedure on many occasions, you should tell your partner immediately *before* you are about to achieve orgasm and request penetration. Practice this on several separate occasions.

Next, ask your partner to penetrate several seconds before you are about to achieve orgasm. The stimulus for orgasm will gradually become his penis and not his hand. In this way, you will be able to achieve an orgasm during intercourse.

To repeat, it is usually important that the above sexual behaviors occur within a committed relationship. Where exploitation surrounds a sexual relationship, negative feelings toward sex are likely to be engendered. In addition, the above suggestions assume that the female is physically normal. Before implementing these procedures, consult a physician to ascertain and treat any physical dysfunctions which may prevent you from experiencing orgasmic pleasure.

IMPOTENCE

Impotence is the inability to create and maintain an erection. It results in unnecessary embarrassment and shame for the male and may involve feelings of rejection in the female. Most males are impotent at some time. For example, during holidays, some males may drink more alcohol than usual. Since alcohol has a depressing effect on the central nervous system, the male may discover (to his alarm) that he cannot get an erection.

The causes of impotence may be physiological or psychological. The holiday example illustrates a physiological cause. In addition, drugs, diabetes, and diseases of the central nervous system may induce impotence. Before implementing a plan to overcome impotence, it is important to rule out any physiological dysfunction. A physician should be consulted if this cause is suspected.

Psychological causes of impotence include worry over factors external to the relationship and anxiety related to an aggressive partner. School failure, death of a sibling or parent, and no insurance on an expensive stereo destroyed by fire are examples of events which may create a depressive mood and induce impotence. This type of impotence usually disappears with the passage of time and the return of more favorable external conditions.

A more frequent cause of impotence is an aggressive partner who can be satisfied through intercourse only. The female constantly communicates her availability and desire for intercourse. She touches her partner frequently. She kisses his cheeks and strokes his legs. He perceives her as always ready for intercourse. He believes that he need only demonstrate the slightest interest in sex to get her in the mood for intercourse.

The sexually aggressive female who is perceived as always ready for intercourse often creates anxiety in her partner. This anxiety will inhibit an erection. For example, if someone were to place the barrel of a shotgun to a male's head and tell him that he must get an erection in 30 seconds or his brains would be splattered, the male would die. Only in situations where pressure, tension, and anxiety are absent can an erection occur.

The problem of impotence becomes compounded when the female restricts the possibilities of her sexual satisfaction to intercourse. Wives of impotent husbands frequently will not allow their partner to stimulate them manually, orally, or through use of an electric vibrator. These females often say "it's not natural." Through blocking other sources of sexual satisfaction, these wives put increased pressure on their husbands to perform with their penis. This is the very condition under which impotence will occur.

To effectively resolve a problem of impotence, four conditions must be met: (1) A physician should be consulted to rule out any possibility of a physiological dysfunction. (2) No intercourse should occur for a period of one month. This condition reduces any pressure on the male to have intercourse. He is assured that he will not have to perform with his penis in the next 30 days. The agreement means that even though the male gets a very strong erection, the couple should not have intercourse. With the pressure to have intercourse removed, the male often experiences no trouble in achieving an erection.

(3) The male must satisfy his partner by means other than intercourse. Manual, oral, or vibratory stimulation are often effective procedures for inducing an enjoyable orgasmic experience. By allowing the male alternative means to satisfy his partner, it is not necessary that he get an erection. This further reduces the anxiety which inhibits erection.

(4) The male must approach his partner four times each week for intercourse for a four-week period. Each time he approaches his partner, she should refuse to have intercourse with him. Under no circumstances should intercourse occur. It is important that the male separate the issue of rejection from the issue of playing the refusal game. His partner is not rejecting him, rather, this game further reduces the pressure on him to have intercourse since his partner is actively refusing to do so.

If there is no physiological base, and procedures usually 2, 3, and 4 are implemented, the problem of impotence will usually disappear. It is interesting to note that impotence is a learned behavior and that it can be unlearned by controlling the conditions under which it does not occur.

PREMATURE EJACULATION

More frequent than impotence is the problem of premature ejaculation, which is defined as an inability to delay ejaculation long enough for the woman to have an orgasm fifty percent of the time (Masters and Johnson, 1970). The uncontrollable, involuntary ejaculation may cause embarrassment, feelings of inadequacy and guilt in the male while the female may experience frustration and resentment toward her partner.

Masters and Johnson (1970) have extended a treatment procedure suggested by Dr. James Semans (1956). They reported successful treatment of 182 (out of 186) cases of premature ejaculation by using this procedure.

The female manually manipulates her partner's penis until he experiences the slightest hint of impending ejaculation. When he alerts her that he is experiencing such a feeling, she squeezes the head of his penis between her thumb and two fingers. A three to four second hard squeeze inhibits the desire to ejaculate. She then resumes manipulation after a thirty-second delay and repeats the procedure three or four times without allowing ejaculation to occur.

After practicing this procedure on different occasions for several days or until the male is able to delay his ejaculation following long periods of manipulation, the treatment for ejaculatory delay during intercourse begins. While the male lies on his back, his partner straddles him and inserts his penis into her vagina. At first, she sits slowly with no pelvic thrusting from either partner. Should the male experience the desire to ejaculate, she should lift from his penis and apply the squeeze technique. After repeated trials, the male is able to experience prolonged penetration without ejaculation. As his ability to control ejaculation increases, pelvic thrusting may begin and other positions adopted as desired.

This procedure requires patience and excellent communication between partners. A more detailed discussion of the procedure can be found in *Understanding Human Sexual Inadequacy* by Belliveau and Richter (1970).

SUMMARY

A sexual problem may be resolved by understanding the causes of the problem and implementing a plan to remove these causes. Differences over frequency of intercourse, lack of orgasm, impotence, and premature ejaculation are among the more frequent sexual concerns of college couples.

BIBLIOGRAPHY

BELL, R. R. Some emerging sexual expectations among women. *Medical Aspects of Human Sexuality*, October, 1967, 65–67, 72.

BELLIVEAU, F. and RICHTER, L. *Understanding human sexual inadequacy*. New York: Bantam Books, Inc., 1970.

"J." *The Sensuous Woman*. New York: Lyle Stuart, 1969.

KNOX, D. *Dr. Knox's Marital Exercise Book*. New York: David McKay Co., Inc., forthcoming.

MACKLIN, E. D. Heterosexual cohabitation among unmarried college students. *The Family Coordinator*, 1972, **21**, 463–72.

MASTERS, W. H. and JOHNSON, V. E. *Human sexual inadequacy*. Boston: Little, Brown, and Co., 1970.

SEMANS, J. H. Premature ejaculation: A new approach. *Southern Medical Journal*, 1956, **49**, 353–57.

Indexes

AUTHOR INDEX

SUBJECT INDEX